FASHIONPEDIA

THE VISUAL DICTIONARY
OF FASHION DESIGN

FASHIONARY

FASHIONARY

ISBN 978-988-13547-6-1
SN FPV161912PBCB

Designed and published in Hong Kong
by Fashionary International Ltd
Printed in China

Fashionpedia is an ongoing project. If you have any feedback, please don't hesitate to send it to
feedback@fashionary.org

☐ @ fashionary
🐦 @ fashionarybook
📷 @ fashionary
📌 @ fashionary

Fashionary Team
2020

CONTENTS

PREFACE

Fashion designers are constantly on the search for inspiration and design possibilities. They also need to communicate with factories and buyers, which requires the use of technical terms and jargon. What fashion professionals really need is a simple yet practical handbook that addresses all their needs in a straightforward, user-friendly manner. All these inspired the birth of *Fashionpedia*, literally a fashion encyclopedia with a wealth of practical information that one needs as a fashion designer.

Simple, informative, portable and elegant, *Fashionpedia* truly embodies our idea and vision of an all-encompassing fashion bible. Here at Fashionary, we understand that visuals and images are the universal language of designers worldwide. Therefore, *Fashionpedia* presents all complex information as easy-to-read infographics. Our carefully curated sections make it easy to navigate, allowing users to quickly locate the information they need. As with our signature line of Fashionary notebooks, *Fashionpedia* also comes in a sleek, compact form for portable, on-the-go use to suit fashion designers' busy lifestyles.

On our quest to create the dream fashion tool book, we have consulted with professionals to ensure all information included in *Fashionpedia* reflects the industry standard. Our design team has dedicated months to perfecting the graphics and layout for the best readability.

'Without foundations, there can be no fashion,' Christian Dior once said. We hope you find *Fashionpedia* as inspirational as we do, and may it become a fundamental and indispensable part of your fashion ambitions.

- Fashionary Team

FASHIONS FADE, STYLE IS ETERNAL.

/ YVES SAINT LAURENT

01 FASHION HISTORY & STYLE

FASHION AND WORLD HISTORY /
FASHION STYLE AND SILHOUETTE

1.1 FASHION AND WORLD HISTORY FROM THE 20TH CENTURY

Coco Chanel once said, *"Fashion is not something that exists in dresses only. Fashion is in the sky, in the street; fashion has to do with ideas, the way we live, what is happening."*
Fashion is a fast-changing concept that connects with everybody's everyday life especially from the 20th century. Styles and ideas became more accessible to fashion designers by improved communication and the media. Fashion is a part of who we are, the way we live, and the times in which we exist. To start off, a timeline is included to show the relationship between the fashion trends and world events from the 20th century, and also the fashion keywords and style icons of the decades.

1900s

The Edwardian Era &
rise of Parisian haute couture

1910s

The Oriental Era &
WWI

FASHION

- **1903**
  Paul Poiret established his
  couture house in Paris

- **1909**
  Condé Nast
  took over Vogue
  magazine.

- **1912**
  'Queen of the Bias Cut' Madeleine
  Vionnet opened her couture house

- **1914**
  Burberry trench
  coat used by the
  British Army
  during WWI

- **CHANEL**
  1909

- **PRADA**
  1912

- Ermenegildo Zegna
  1910

- BALENCIAGA
  1914

- Heinrich Stoll invented the
  flat bed purl knitting
  machine

- Designer Mariano
  Fortuny patented his
  pleat-setting
  technique

- First modern bra design
  patented in the United States

- Spiers invented the circular
  bed purl knitting machine

- Gideon Sundback
  patented the
  modern zipper

POPULAR CULTURE

POST-
IMPRESSIONISM &
ART NOUVEAU

CONSTRUCTIVISM

FAUVISM &
GERMAN
EXPRESSIONISM

DADA

ABSTRACT
ART & CUBISM

- First Silent Movie:
  The Great Train Robbery

WORLD

WORLD WAR I
1914-1918

 Albert Einstein
published the Theory of
Relativity and introduced
the famous equation,
$E = mc^2$

 First AM radio factory opened

 Ernest Rutherford, Father of Nuclear Physics,
theorized that atoms have their charge
concentrated in a very small nucleus

KEYWORDS & STYLE ICONS

Bishop's Sleeve   BOA   Cabochon

Camiknickers   Collarette   Covert Coat

Dog-collar Neckline   Duster

Lingerie Look   Negligee   Panama Hat

Pegged Trousers   Pompadour

Racer   S-bend Corset

Style Icons
Gibson Girl, Camille Clifford

Brassiere   Cloche   Jupe-culottes

Minaret Tunic   Oriental Opulence

Peter Pan Collar

Style Icons
Duff Gordon, Gabrielle Dorziat

1920s
The Roaring Twenties

1930s
Hollywood's influence & WWII

FASHION

- **1926**
  Coco Chanel published a picture of a 'little black dress' in American Vogue

- **1937**
  Elsa Schiaparelli designed the 'Lobster Dress' with artist Salvador Dalí

- GUCCI
  1921
- BOSS
  1924
- Salvatore Ferragamo
  1928

- Development of metal hooks and eyes

- Wallace Carothers and DuPont Labs invented nylon (polymer 6.6)

POPULAR CULTURE

ART DECO

SURREALISM

- 'IT'

- Morning Glory
- Camille

- Gone with the Wind

- The Kid

- Metropolis

- Shanghai Express · Modern Times

- The Wizard of Oz

WORLD

$ Black Thursday & the start of the Great Depression

WORLD
1939-19

Philo Farnsworth invented the first all-electronic television system

BBC
BBC started the world's first television broadcasting servic

KEYWORDS & STYLE ICONS

Art Deco	Balloon Shoes	Blanket Cloth
Cloverleaf Lapel	Clutch Coat	Corselette
Flapper	Handkerchief Skirt	Jabot Blouse
Oxford Bag	Plus Fours	Polo Shirt
Raccoon Skin Coat	Singlet	Slip

Style Icons
Zelda Fitzgerald, Louise Brooks, Coco Chanel, Rudolph Valentino, Elsa Schiaparelli, Pola Negri, Clara Bow

Batwing Sleeve	Bias Cut	Blade Cut Suit
Drape Cut Suit	Guards Coat	Huaraches
Lido Shoes	Loafers	Mess Jacket
Monk	Pagoda Sleeve	Seersucker
Toy Hat	Tyrolean	Weskit

Style Icons
Greta Garbo, Bette Davis, Marlene Dietrich, Wallis Simpson, Clark Gable, Katharine Hepburn

1940s

The era of utility clothing

1950s

Rise of ready-to-wear
(prêt-à-porter)

- **1942**
American ready-to-wear industry developed in response to wartime clothing regulations and the American look was created

We Can Do It!

- **1943**
First fashion week: New York Fashion Week

- **1947**
Christian Dior created the "New Look"

· Dior
1946

- **1952**
Cristóbal Balenciaga designed the sack line

· GIVENCHY
1952

· pierre cardin
1950

· MISSONI
1953

- **1955**
Marilyn Monroe's wind-blown white dress

- First wrinkle-resistant finishing created
- Commercial use of artificial silk in women's lingerie and hosiery
- Fiber reactive dye invented
- First commercial polyester fiber production by DuPont

POP ART

ABSTRACT EXPRESSIONISM

GABLE·LAMARR
· Comrade X

· Casablanca

· Gilda

● Elvis Presley's Elvis Presley (album)

PRESLEY

· Roman Holiday

○ **VIETNAM WAR**
1955-1979

○ **COLD WAR**
1947-1991

Atomic bombings of Hiroshima and Nagasaki

POST-WAR BABY BOOM

$ Post-war economic boom

THE SPACE AGE

Atom	Battle Jacket	Bikini
Bold Look	Bomber Jacket	
Chinos	Cigarette Silhouette	
Duffle Coat	Dungarees	New Look
Prêt-à-porter	Pullman Robe	Spool Torso

Style Icons
Ingrid Bergman, Fred Astaire, Rita Hayworth, Hedy Lamarr, Barbara "Babe" Paley, Diana Vreeland

A-line	Ballet Slippers	Balmacaan
Bermuda Shorts	Capri Pants	Circle Skirt
Cocoon Silhouette	Flare Coat	H-line
Ivy League Style	Pedal Pushers	
Shirtwaister	Stilettos	Teddy Boys
Toppers	Trapeze Line	Y-line

Style Icons
Audrey Hepburn, James Dean, Bettie Page, Grace Kelly, Elizabeth Taylor, Marilyn Monroe, Elvis Presley

1960s

The Flower Power Era & ethnic folkloric

1970s

The 'Me' Decade & rise of anti-fashion

FASHION

- **1964**
  André Courrèges showed his Space Age collection in Paris
  - **1965**
    Yves Saint Laurent dress inspired by artist Piet Mondrian

  - **1966** Twiggy declared as 'The Face of 1966'

- **1970**
  Vivienne Westwood created punk fashion

  - **1977**
    The Sex Pistols perfo 'God Save the Queen' wearing Westwood

- **1973**
  Kansai Yamamoto designed costumes for David Bowie's Ziggy Stardust Tour

  - **1974**
    Beverly Johnson as the first black model on the cover of American Vogue

- VALENTINO
  1960

- RALPH LAUREN
  1967

- YVESSAINTLAURENT
  1961

- Rise of Velcro (hook-and-loop fasterners) in fashion industry

- Permanent-press fabric invented

- VERSACE
  1978

- GIORGIO ARMANI
  1975

MINIMALISM

OP ART

POPULAR CULTURE

The Beatles' Sgt. Pepper's Lonely Hearts Club Band

- Annie Hall

- Breakfast at Tiffany's

- 2001: A Space Odyssey

- Saturday Night Fever

WORLD

VIETNAM WAR
1955-1979

COLD WAR
1947-1991

 $ 1970s Recession

🌙 MOON LANDING

Audio cassette invented

Walkm invent

KEYWORDS & STYLE ICONS

Afron	Baby Doll Gown	Beehive Hairstyle
Bell Button	Broomsticks	
Carnaby Street Look	Chelsea Boots	
Go-go Boots	Hiphugger	Maxi & Midi Skirt
Mini Skirt	Mod Look	Nehru Suit

Baggies	Dressing-gown Coat	
Duvet Coat	Folklorica	Gatsby Suit
Gauchos	Glam & Glitter Rock Style	
Gypsy Style	Hippie Style	Hot Pants
Platform Shoes	Punk Look	Turtlesuit

Style Icons
Mary Quant, Twiggy, Penelope Tree, Yoko Ono, Cher, Diana Ross, Brian Jones, The Beatles, Jacqueline Kennedy, Jane Birkin, Grace Coddington, Jean Shrimpton

Style Icons
Pam Grier, Sid Vicious, Farrah Fawcet, Beverly Johnson, Bianca Jagger, Iman, Debbie Harry, Olivia Newton-John, Jane Fonda, Ali Macgraw, Jerry Hall, Patti Smith, Diane Keaton

1980s

Power dressing &
the yuppie era

1990s

Era of personal expression

- **1981**
  Japanese
  Deconstructionists
  showed in Paris

- **1986**
  A group of Belgian avant-garde fashion designers -
  The 'Antwerp Six' showed their collection in London

- **1998**
  Sex and the City
  (TV series) first
  screened

- **1981**
  Dynasty (TV series)
  first screened

- **1993**
  Kate Moss in Calvin Klein
  underwear campaign

- **1990**
  Madonna wore
  the cone bra
  designed by Jean
  Paul Gaultier on
  Blond Ambition
  World Tour

- DOLCE & GABBANA
  1985

- **DKNY**
  1984

- Development of digital textile
  printing technology

NEO EXPRESSIONISM

VIRTUAL ART

Michael Jackson's
Thriller

Nirvana's Nevermind

Spice Girls' Spice

- E.T. the Extra-Terrestrial

- Pretty Woman

$ Goldilocks Economy

COLD WAR
1947-1991

IBM
MS-DOS &
first IBM-PC
invented

M First commercially
available cell phone
invented by Motorola

**The World Wide Web and Internet
protocol (HTTP) and WWW language
(HTML) created

- Google
  1998

 Apple Macintosh invented

Aerobics Craze	B-Boys	Bolla
Deconstruction	Ferrule	
Miami Vice Loop	Pouf Dress	
Power Dressing	Rockability	Romantique
Shell Toes	Skin Head	Skinny Tie

Anti-fashion	Board Shorts	Bogolanfini Cloth
Boxer Briefs	Caesar Chic	Casual Chic
Cyberstyle	Grunge	Hipster	Minimalism
Racer	Slope	Tattoo & Body Piercing
Technotextile	Workout Clothing	

Style Icons
Diana Spencer, Madonna, Michael Jackson,
David Bowie, Grace Jones, Prince, Boy George,
Demi Moore, Cyndi Lauper, George Michael

Style Icons
Kate Moss, Courtney Love, Kurt Cobain, Naomi Campbell,
Isabella Blow, Liz Tilberis, Linda Evangelista,
Cindy Crawford, Heidi Klum

2000s

Rise of "Fast Fashion"

2010s

Rise of "Slow Fashion"

FASHION

- **2002**
  Takashi Murakami x
  Louis Vuitton collection

- **2005**
  Alexander McQueen
  used hologram of
  Kate Moss in his Fall
  2006 Fashion Show

- **2007**
  Anya Hindmarch
  designed the global
  sell-out tote bag
  'I'm Not a Plastic Bag'

- **2010**
  Burberry streamed its A/W 2010
  show live in 3D in six cities, allowing
  the audience to pre-order directly
  from the catwalk

 Rise of online shopping

Rise of sustainable and eco fashion

POPULAR CULTURE

 OutKast's Speakerboxxx /
The Love Below

● Lady Gaga's The Fame

- Factory Girl

WORLD

○ **9/11 ATTACK & WAR ON TERROR**
2001-present

$ Great Recession

 iPhone launched
2007

● **twitter**
2006

● **Google +**
2011

● **You Tube**
2005

● **facebook**
2005

● **Instagram**
2010

KEYWORDS & STYLE ICONS

| 1960s Revival | Absurdist | Admiral Jacket |

| Boho (bohemian) Style | Boyfriend Style |

| Fast Fashion | Green Fashion | Shrunken Look |

| Slim-fit Suit | Smart Fabric | Sustainable Fabric |

| Trash Fashion (Trashion) | Tribal Look | Y2K Fashion |

Style Icons
Sienna Miller, Chloë Sevigny, Nicole Richie, Sarah Jessica Parker,
Lady Gaga, Mary-Kate And Ashley Olsen, Rihanna, Alexa Chung, Hedi
Slimane, Carine Roitfeld, Franca Sozzani, Anna Wintour, Michelle
Obama, Gisele Bündchen

1.2 FASHION STYLE AND SILHOUETTE

Fashion styles and popular apparel trends are constantly in flux, and fashion in the West in particular has experienced continual upheavals and major changes. Popular fads have included such fashion statements as rear-enhancing bustles, short flapper dresses, wide-leg bell bottoms, and deliberately ripped jeans. These and other major fashion styles make up the fascinating history of fashion.

FASHION STYLES IN HISTORY

——— Egyptian ———

🕐 3100 - 332 BC

📍 Egypt

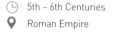

——— Byzantine ———

🕐 5th – 6th Centuries

📍 Roman Empire

——— Medieval ———

🕐 5th – 15th Centuries

📍 Europe

——— Elizabethan ———

🕐 1550s – 1600s

📍 England

——— Rococo ———

🕐 1750 – 1775

📍 Europe and North America

— Empire / Regency —

🕐 1790s – 1820s

📍 Western and Central Europe

——— Victorian ———

🕐 1830s – 1900s

📍 British Empire

——— Gibson Girl ———

🕐 1890s – 1910s

📍 United States

——— Sailor ———
Breton stripes

🕐 1910s

📍 France

——— The 20s ———

🕐 1920s

📍 Europe

——— Flapper ———

🕐 1920s

📍 Europe

——— Art Deco ———

🕐 1920s

📍 Europe

— Hollywood Starlet —

🕐 1920s – 1940s

📍 Europe and
United States

——— The 30s ———

🕐 1930s

📍 United States

——— The 40s ———

🕐 1940s

📍 Europe and
United States

——— Military ———

🕐 1940s

📍 Global

——— Pin-up Girl ———

🕐 1940s – 1950s

📍 United States

——— New Look ———

🕐 1940s – 1950s

📍 France

——— Fetish ———

——— The 50s ———

——— Teddy Girl ———

🕐 1940s - 1950s

📍 England and
United States

🕐 1950s

📍 Europe and
United States

🕐 1950s

📍 England

——— Tropical ———

——— Preppy ———

——— Beatnik ———

🕐 1950s

📍 United States

🕐 1950s

📍 United States

🕐 1950s – mid-1960s

📍 United States

———— The 60s ————

🕐 1960s

📍 Europe and
United States

———— Mondrian ————

🕐 1960s

📍 France

———— Op Art ————

🕐 1960s

📍 Europe

———— Space Age ————

🕐 1960s

📍 Europe

———— Jackie ————

🕐 1960s

📍 United States

———— Hippie ————

🕐 Mid-1960s

📍 United States

————— The 70s —————

🕐 1970s

📍 Europe and
United States

————— Annie Hall —————

🕐 1970s

📍 United States

————— Punk —————

🕐 1970s - 1980s

📍 England

————— Lolita —————

🕐 Late 1970s

📍 Japan

— 80s Power Dressing —

🕐 1980s

📍 United States

— Flashdance / Disco —

🕐 1980s

📍 United States

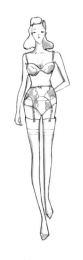

———— Goth ————

🕐 1980s
📍 Europe

———— Lingerie ————
as outerwear

🕐 1980s
📍 Europe

— Modern Equestrian —

🕐 1980s
📍 Europe

———— Kitsch ————

🕐 1980s - 1990s
📍 Europe

———— Minimalist ————

🕐 1990s
📍 United States

———— Casual Chic ————

🕐 1990s - 2000s
📍 Global

STYLE BY ETHNIC

——— Amish ———

🕐 1690s - Present
📍 United States

——— Folklore ———
brought to high fashion

🕐 1970s
📍 Europe

——— Qipao / Chinese ———

🕐 1920s - Present
📍 China

—— Native American / ——
Indian
📍 North America

—— Kimono / Japanese ——

📍 Japan

——— Gypsy / Romani ———

📍 Europe and
United States

MEN'S STYLE

—— Regency ——
Beau Brummell

🕐 1790s - 1820s

📍 Japan

—— Edwardian ——

🕐 1900s

📍 United Kingdom

—— Zoot Suit ——

🕐 1940s

📍 United States

—— Cowboy ——

🕐 Mid-20th Century

📍 America

—— Teddy Boy ——

🕐 1950s

📍 United Kingdom

—— Ivy League ——

🕐 Late 1950s

📍 United States

——— 60s Mod ———

🕐 1960s
📍 England

——— Hippie ———

🕐 Mid-1960s
📍 United States

——— Punk ———

🕐 1970s - 1980s
📍 England

——— 80s Heavy Metal ———

🕐 1980s
📍 United States

——— Hip-hop ———

🕐 1980s
📍 United States

——— Grunge ———

🕐 1990s
📍 United States

SILHOUETTE & LINE

A-line

H-line

I-line / Column / Shift

V-line

X-line

Y-line

Curved Line

Empire Line

Princess Line

Asymmetric Silhouette

Ballerina Silhouette

Ballgown Silhouette

Balloon Silhouette

Barrel Silhouette

Bell Silhouette

Bustle / S-bend
Silhouette

Cocoon
Silhouette

Fit and Flare /
Skater Silhouette

Flare and Tight
Silhouette

Flare and Tube
Silhouette

Hobble
Silhouette

Hourglass
Silhouette

Mermaid
Silhouette

Off-shoulder
Silhouette

Peg-top
Silhouette

Sheath
Silhouette

Spindle
Silhouette

Tiered
Silhouette

Trapeze / Tent
Silhouette

Trumpet
Silhouette

I COME FROM A DIFFERENT ERA AND I DESIGN CLOTHES FOR OUR ERA. I THINK OF PEOPLE I WANT TO DRESS WHEN I DESIGN.

/ ALEXANDER MCQUEEN

02 APPAREL

———

JACKET / COAT AND OUTERWEAR / SHIRT / BLOUSE AND OTHER TOPS / DRESS / VEST / SWEATER AND CARDIGAN / DENIM AND JEANS / PANTS / SKIRT / JUMPSUIT AND OVERALL / SUIT / SLEEPWEAR AND NIGHTWEAR / UNDERWEAR

2.1 JACKET

The term *jacket* is derived from the French word *jacquette*, which comes from the Middle French word *jacquet*, meaning a small or lightweight tunic. A jacket is commonly defined as an outer garment for the upper body which reaches the mid-torso. Typically tailored with sleeves and a fastening on the front or slightly towards the side, jackets are generally lighter, more form-fitting and less insulating than coats.

JACKET DETAILS & MEASUREMENTS

APPAREL

Jacket / Coat / Shirt / Blouse / Dress / Vest / Sweater & Cardigan / Denim / Pants / Skirt / Jumpsuit / Suit / Sleepwear / Underwear

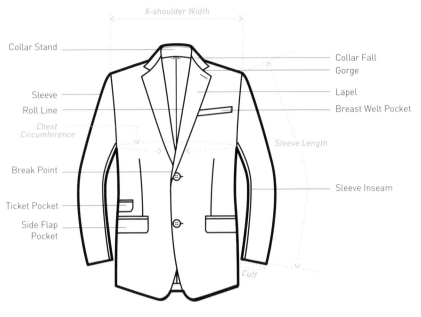

- X-shoulder Width
- Collar Stand
- Collar Fall
- Gorge
- Sleeve
- Lapel
- Roll Line
- Breast Welt Pocket
- Chest Circumference
- Sleeve Length
- Break Point
- Sleeve Inseam
- Ticket Pocket
- Side Flap Pocket
- Cuff

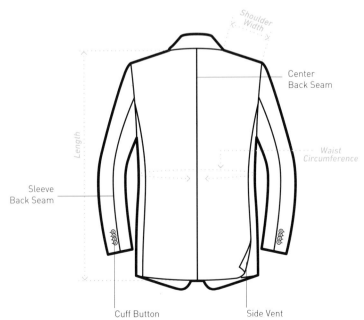

- Shoulder Width
- Center Back Seam
- Length
- Waist Circumference
- Sleeve Back Seam
- Cuff Button
- Side Vent

Tailored Jacket
always with matching pants

Blazer
without matching pants

Dinner Jacket / Tuxedo
dinner jacket for Black Tie

Dinner Jacket / Tuxedo
(For White Tie)

White Tie, also known as full evening
dress, is the most formal of all dress
codes in Western menswear tradition.
It is typically only worn after 6pm
for ceremonial functions, such as
presidential dinners, state occasions,
evening weddings or very formal balls.

Mess Jacket / Eton Jacket

Single-breasted Jacket

Double-breasted Jacket

35

APPAREL

Jacket / Coat / Shirt / Blouse / Dress / Vest / Sweater & Cardigan / Denim / Pants / Skirt / Jumpsuit / Suit / Sleepwear / Underwear

Hunting Jacket

Smoking Jacket

Smoking jackets are designed to be worn while smoking pipes, cigars or cigarettes as a means of catching falling ashes and absorbing the smell of the smoke to protect the clothing underneath. One of the most famous smoking jacket wearers is Hugh Hefner, founder of Playboy magazine. He owns over 200 different smoking jackets / pajama tops that are custom-made for him.

Edwardian Jacket

Spencer Jacket

Norfolk Jacket

Monkey Jacket

Horse Riding Jacket /
Show Jacket /
Equestrian Jacket

Safari Jacket

Biker Jacket

Flight Jacket

M-65 Field Jacket

ALS/92 Field Jacket Liner

liner for M-65 Field Jacket

N-3B Flight Parka

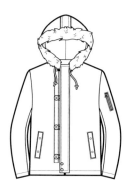

N-2B Flight Jacket

MA-1 Bomber Jacket

Torero Jacket / Matador Jacket / Chaqueta

The traditional clothing worn by Spanish bullfighters in the bullring, the matador jacket is known as the 'traje de luces' in Spanish, meaning 'suit of lights', due to the sequins and shiny gold or silver threads used to embellish the garment. Commonly short and rigid, the chaqueta is enforced with attachments at the upper shoulder, allowing unimpeded movement of the arm. It usually comes in red, black, green, blue or white, but never yellow, which is considered an unlucky color by toreros who are keenly superstitious.

Majorette Jacket

Bolero Jacket

Tyrolean Jacket

Nehru Jacket

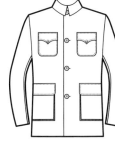

Mao Jacket

Shirt Jacket

Harrington Jacket

Denim Jacket

Lumber Jacket

Letter Jacket / Varsity Jacket / Baseball Jacket

Originating from high school and college traditions in the United States, letter jackets were worn by students to demonstrate school and team pride and to display personal athletic achievements. They are typically adorned with a chenille varsity letter patch on the left chest which usually represents the first letter or initial of the high school or college, hence the name 'letter jacket'.

Windbreaker

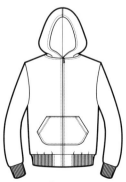

Hoodie / Zip-up Jacket

Down Jacket

APPAREL

Jacket / Coat / Shirt / Blouse / Dress / Vest / Sweater & Cardigan / Denim / Pants / Skirt / Jumpsuit / Suit / Sleepwear / Underwear

Sleeveless Jacket

Peplum Jacket

Belted Jacket

Blouson Jacket

Roomy Jacket

Midriff Jacket / Cropped Jacket

Western Jacket

Cocoon Jacket

Oversized Jacket

2.2 COAT AND OUTERWEAR

One of the earliest clothing category words found in English history, coats can be traced back to the Middle Ages. Worn by both men and women either for warmth, fashion or both, a coat is typically defined as a long garment with long sleeves and an open front, which is usually fastened with buttons, toggles, hook-and-eye fasteners, a zipper, a waist belt or any combination of the aforementioned items. It may also feature a collar, cuff straps and shoulder epaulettes.

COAT DETAILS & MEASUREMENTS

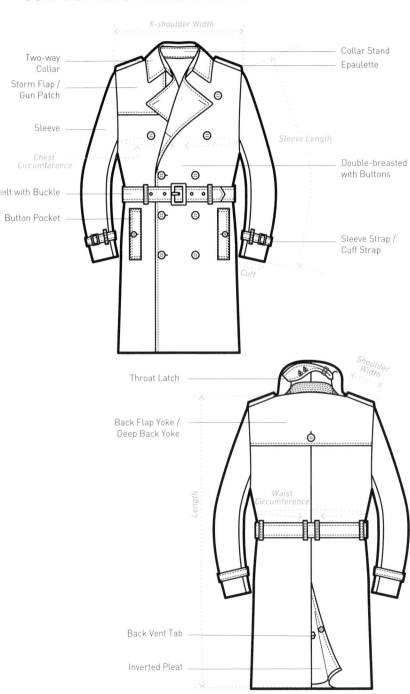

X-shoulder Width

Two-way Collar

Storm Flap / Gun Patch

Sleeve

Chest Circumference

Belt with Buckle

Button Pocket

Collar Stand

Epaulette

Sleeve Length

Double-breasted with Buttons

Sleeve Strap / Cuff Strap

Cuff

Throat Latch

Back Flap Yoke / Deep Back Yoke

Shoulder Width

Length

Waist Circumference

Back Vent Tab

Inverted Pleat

LENGTHS OF COATS

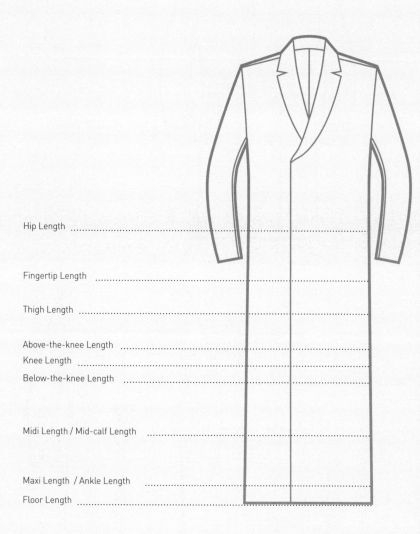

Hip Length

Fingertip Length

Thigh Length

Above-the-knee Length
Knee Length
Below-the-knee Length

Midi Length / Mid-calf Length

Maxi Length / Ankle Length
Floor Length

43

APPAREL

Jacket / **Coat** / Shirt / Blouse / Dress / Vest / Sweater & Cardigan / Denim / Pants / Skirt / Jumpsuit / Suit / Sleepwear / Underwear

Inverness Coat

no full cape at the back

British Warm Overcoat

originally made from
fleece-like Melton cloth

Chesterfield Coat

A long and tailored overcoat often with a velvet
collar, the Chesterfield coat was introduced
alongside the lounge suit as an alternative
option to highly structural coats, such as the
frock overcoat, which heavily suppress the
waist with its waist seam.

Polo Coat

originally made from camel hair

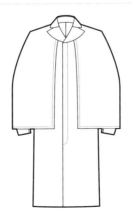

Ulster Coat

the cape was removed after the Edwardian
period, often double-breasted

Ulsterette

a lightweight version
of Ulster Coat

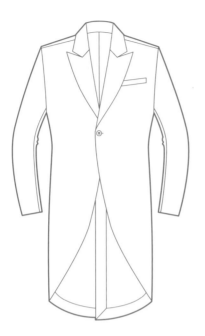

Balmacaan
made from rough woolen cloth

Guards Coat
has a half belt at the back

Morning Coat

The formal dress code for daytime, the morning coat was traditionally worn by gentlemen in the 19th century during morning horseback riding exercises, from which it got its name.

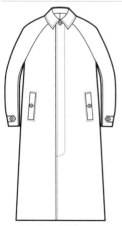

Mackintosh Raincoat
made from rubberized or
rubber laminated material

Frock Coat

Redingote

Full Trench Coat

Clutch Coat

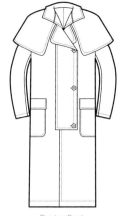

Duster Coat

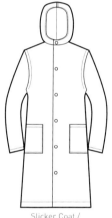

Slicker Coat /
Sou'wester Coat

Duffle Coat

Skating Coat

Tent Coat

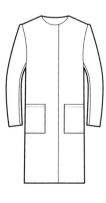

Straight Coat

Princess Line Coat

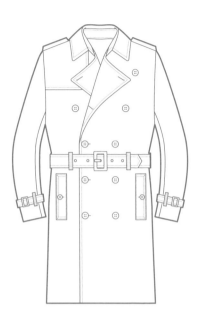

Trench Coat

Originally invented by the British for military purposes, the trench coat became a popular item of clothing after it was introduced to the public post World War I, and was subsequently revolutionized by the British luxury fashion house Burberry. Thomas Burberry, British clothier and founder of Burberry, developed a type of novel wool material called gabardine, which is rip-resistant, virtually creaseproof and processed chemically to be water-repellent, yet remains porous and offers good ventilation for cool and comfortable wear. Gabardine was first used in Burberry trench coats which have since then become a fashion classic.

Belted Coat   Wrap Coat   Cocoon Coat

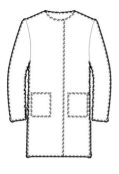

Teddy Bear Coat / Fur Coat

Reefer Coat
for officers only and usually has gold
buttons and epaulettes

Pea Coat

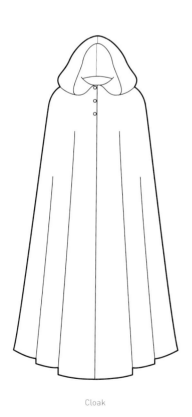

Cloak

Cape Coat / Mantle Coat

Poncho

Car Coat

Clasp Coat

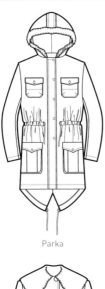

Parka

Cossack Coat

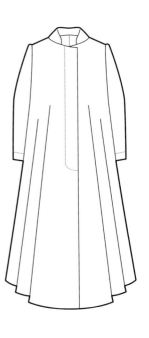

Opera Coat

2.3 **SHIRT**

The oldest preserved item of clothing in the world is a linen shirt found in a First Dynasty Egyptian tomb at Tarkan, tracing back to around 3000 BC. Even as recent as the late 19th century, it was still considered improper in Western dress code to wear a shirt on its own with nothing on top of it.

SHIRT DETAILS & MEASUREMENTS

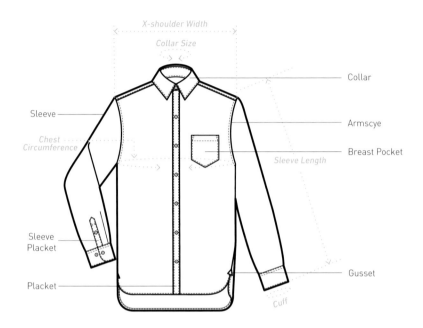

X-shoulder Width

Collar Size

Collar

Sleeve

Armscye

Chest Circumference

Breast Pocket

Sleeve Length

Sleeve Placket

Placket

Gusset

Cuff

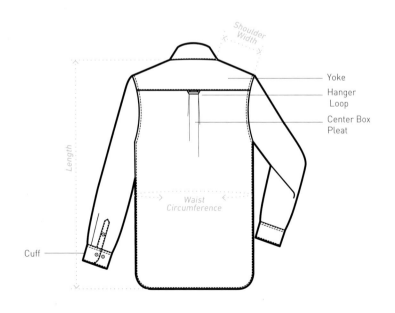

Shoulder Width

Yoke

Hanger Loop

Center Box Pleat

Length

Waist Circumference

Cuff

TYPES OF SHIRT SLEEVES

APPAREL

Jacket / Coat / **Shirt** / Blouse / Dress / Vest / Sweater & Cardigan / Denim / Pants / Skirt / Jumpsuit / Suit / Sleepwear / Underwear

SLEEVE LENGTHS

TYPES OF SLEEVES

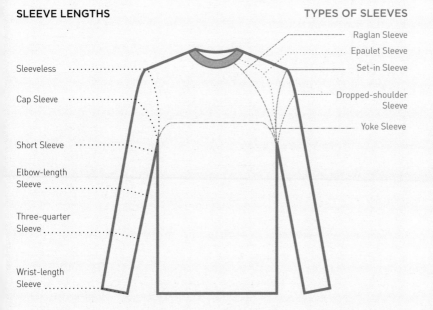

Sleeveless

Cap Sleeve

Short Sleeve

Elbow-length Sleeve

Three-quarter Sleeve

Wrist-length Sleeve

Raglan Sleeve

Epaulet Sleeve

Set-in Sleeve

Dropped-shoulder Sleeve

Yoke Sleeve

WOVEN SHIRTS

Button-down Shirt

A button-down shirt is a shirt with its collar having the ends fastened to the shirt with buttons.
The button-down shirt was first introduced by John Brooks in 1896, who was inspired by polo players' shirt, as he noticed that polo shirt had sewn buttons to keep the collars fastened to prevent them from flapping around. Now this style is still considered as a more casual or sporty style, especially outside America.

Shirt

Cleric Shirt

Ascot Shirt   Pullover Shirt   Dress Shirt / Tuxedo Shirt

Epaulette Shirt

Fitted Shirt

Open Collar Shirt

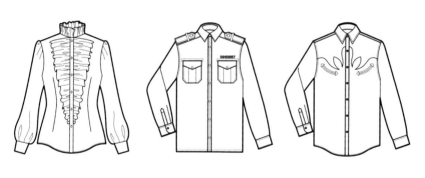

Habit Shirt

Military Shirt

Western Shirt

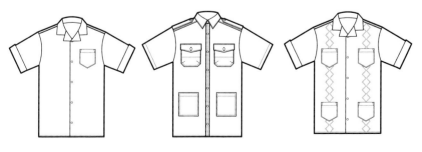

Camp Shirt

Work Shirt

Guayabera Shirt

Zip Front Shirt

Clergy Shirt

Baker's Shirt

Cavalry Shirt

Safari Shirt

A variation of the safari jacket (also known as a bush jacket), the safari shirt was originally intended for wear during African bush safaris, subsequently popularized by Ernest Hemingway in the 1950s and becoming an item of mainstream casual clothing. Designed with many pockets, which can be used for carrying film, lenses, flashes and various small photographic equipment, the safari shirt is especially popular amongst photographers.

Middy Shirt

55

APPAREL

Jacket / Coat / **Shirt** / Blouse / Dress / Vest / Sweater & Cardigan / Denim / Pants / Skirt / Jumpsuit / Suit / Sleepwear / Underwear

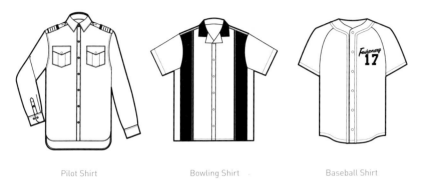

Pilot Shirt   Bowling Shirt   Baseball Shirt

Kurta Shirt   Nehru Shirt   Trapeze Shirt

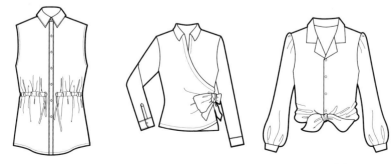

Drawstring Shirt   Wrap Shirt   Tie Waist Shirt

JERSEY SHIRTS

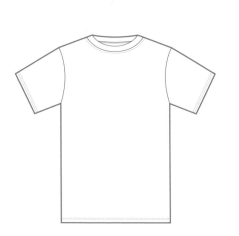

Raglan T-shirt /
Baseball T-shirt

T-Shirt

T-shirts were first issued by the U.S. Navy as undergarments sometime between the 1898 Spanish-American War and 1913. Veterans were commonly spotted wearing T-shirts with their uniform trousers as casual outfits after World War II. They were popularized by Marlon Brando, who wore one in the movie *A Streetcar Named Desire* in 1951, consequently cementing their status as fashion garments.

American Football T-shirt

Rugby Shirt   Polo Shirt   Zip Polo Shirt

APPAREL

Jacket / Coat / **Shirt** / Blouse / Dress / Vest / Sweater & Cardigan / Denim / Pants / Skirt / Jumpsuit / Suit / Sleepwear / Underwear

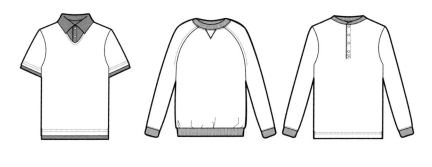

Double T-shirt

Sweatshirt

Henley Shirt

Cropped T-shirt

One-shoulder T-shirt

Sailor Shirt / Basque Shirt

Draped T-shirt

Tunic T-shirt

Tunic Polo Shirt

2.4 BLOUSE AND OTHER TOPS

A blouse is a type of loose-fitting garment for the upper body, conventionally gathered at the waist for a loose-hanging silhouette. Formerly referring to the traditional style worn by peasants, workmen, artists, women and children, the term nowadays broadly applies to women's or girls' dress shirts, and can occasionally describe loose-fitting men's shirts.

BLOUSE DETAILS & MEASUREMENTS

APPAREL

Jacket / Coat / Shirt / **Blouse** / Dress / Vest / Sweater & Cardigan / Denim / Pants / Skirt / Jumpsuit / Suit / Sleepwear / Underwear

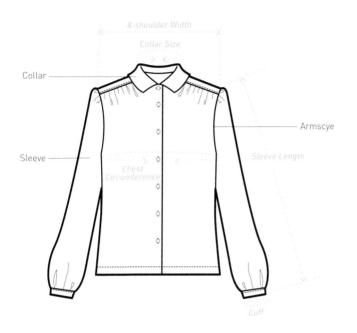

Collar

Sleeve

Armscye

X-shoulder Width

Collar Size

Chest Circumference

Sleeve Length

Cuff

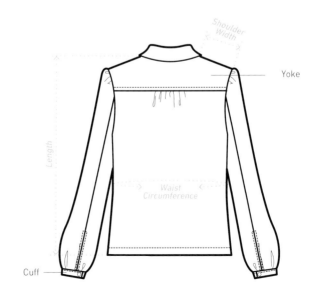

Yoke

Cuff

Shoulder Width

Length

Waist Circumference

Basic Blouse

Tuxedo Blouse

Peasant Blouse

Tie Neck Blouse / Bow Blouse

Tie Waist Blouse

Sash Blouse

Drawstring Blouse

Pullover Blouse

Surplice Blouse

APPAREL

Jacket / Coat / Shirt / **Blouse** / Dress / Vest / Sweater & Cardigan / Denim / Pants / Skirt / Jumpsuit / Suit / Sleepwear / Underwear

Peplum Blouse

Blouson Blouse

Balkan Blouse

Off-the-shoulder Blouse /
Bardot Blouse

Smock Blouse

Poet Blouse

Cut with a loose fit with billowy full bishop sleeves, the
poet blouse is usually adorned with large ruffles at the
collar, front and cuffs. Also dubbed the 'pirate shirt', it
is often matched with accessories or items of clothing
traditionally associated with pirates, such as a wide belt.
When the *Pirates of the Caribbean* adventure movie series
was first released in 2003, poet blouses became a core
theme of the wave of pirate-related fashion trends that
ensued.

Midriff Blouse

Mandarin Blouse

Victorian Blouse

Jabot Blouse

Prairie Blouse

Gibson Blouse

The Gibson blouse is styled with gathered puff sleeves, pleats at the shoulder and a gathered back yoke to help create a curvy silhouette. It was named after the 1900s style icon, Gibson Girl, which was created by artist Charles Gibson. Gibson Girl came to represent the American beauty of the time. When paired with a bustled walking skirt, a full upswept hairdo and a large touring hat, it epitomizes the Gibson Girl style.

Gaucho Blouse

Pirate Blouse

Belted Blouse

Cossack Blouse

Over Blouse

Tunic Blouse

OTHER TOPS

Tank Top

Ballet Top / Wrap Top

Halterneck Top

Shell Top

Camisole

Off-the-shoulder Top / Bardot Top

Cold-shoulder Top

One-shoulder Top

Cropped Top / Midriff Top

Bra Top / Brassiere Top / Sports Bra / Athletic Bra

Tube Top

Bandeau Top

2.5 DRESS

A dress is an item of clothing comprising a bodice and an attached skirt, the hemline of which may vary depending on the fashion trend, occasion, and the wearer's modesty or personal preference. In traditional Western culture, dresses are more commonly worn by females, and a style-appropriate dress is often a mandatory part of Western formal dress codes for women. Dresses are popular for special occasions, such as weddings, balls or proms, for which they are considered the de facto standard female attire.

DRESS DETAILS & MEASUREMENTS

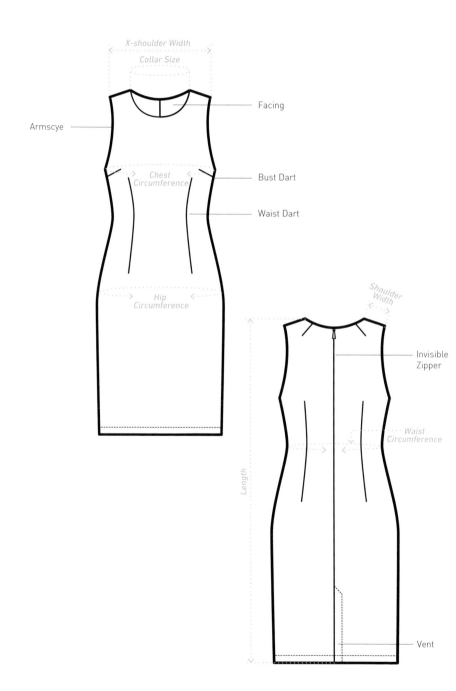

X-shoulder Width

Collar Size

Facing

Armscye

Chest Circumference

Bust Dart

Waist Dart

Hip Circumference

Shoulder Width

Invisible Zipper

Waist Circumference

Length

Vent

APPAREL

Jacket / Coat / Shirt / Blouse / **Dress** / Vest / Sweater & Cardigan / Denim / Pants / Skirt / Jumpsuit / Suit / Sleepwear / Underwear

LENGTHS AND FULLNESS OF DRESS

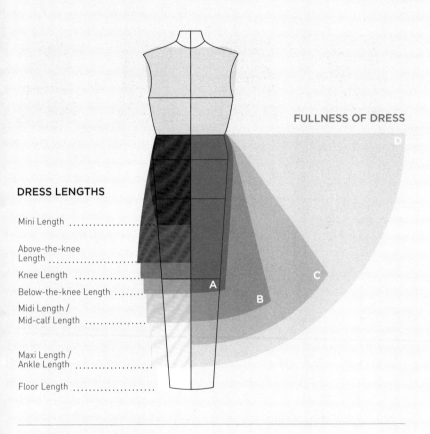

FULLNESS OF DRESS

DRESS LENGTHS

Mini Length ....

Above-the-knee
Length ....

Knee Length ....

Below-the-knee Length ....

Midi Length /
Mid-calf Length ....

Maxi Length /
Ankle Length ....

Floor Length ....

FULLNESS OF DRESS

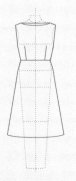

A Pencil Dress   **B** A-line Dress   **C** Semi-circular Dress   **D** Circular Dress

WAISTLINE TYPES

Natural Waistline

Empire Waistline

Dropped Waistline

Basque Waistline

WOVEN DRESSES

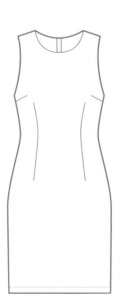

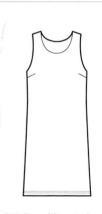
Shift Dress / Chemise Dress

Sheath Dress

A sheath dress is a relatively unembellished dress that fits closely to the body contours, typically of knee length or lower-thigh length as opposed to many cocktail dresses and longer ballroom gowns.

A-line Dress

APPAREL

Jacket / Coat / Shirt / Blouse / **Dress** / Vest / Sweater & Cardigan / Denim / Pants / Skirt / Jumpsuit / Suit / Sleepwear / Underwear

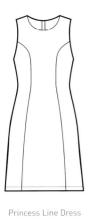

Princess Line Dress

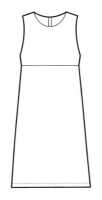

Empire Line Dress

Strap Dress

Trapeze Dress / Tent Dress

Bodycon Dress

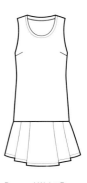

Dropped Waist Dress

Flared Dress / Skater Dress

Tiered Dress

Slip Dress

Tube Dress /
Strapless Dress

Halterneck Dress

Pinafore Dress /
Apron Dress

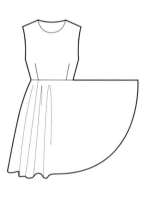

Circular Dress

Peplum Dress

Handkerchief
Hem Dress

Sack Dress

Tunic Dress

Babydoll Dress

APPAREL

Jacket / Coat / Shirt / Blouse / **Dress** / Vest / Sweater & Cardigan / Denim / Pants / Skirt / Jumpsuit / Suit / Sleepwear / Underwear

Panel Dress /
Hourglass Dress

Off-the-shoulder Dress /
Bardot Dress

Coat Dress

Corset Dress

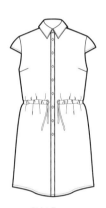

Shirt Dress

House Dress

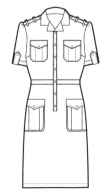

Safari Dress

Bib Dress

Bubble Dress

Smock Dress

Cape Dress

Gymslip

commonly seen as part of
a girl's school uniform

Tutu Dress

Worn for ballet performances, a tutu dress
consists of a basque and a skirt of single or
multiple layers.

Pleated Dress

73

APPAREL

Jacket / Coat / Shirt / Blouse / **Dress** / Vest / Sweater & Cardigan / Denim / Pants / Skirt / Jumpsuit / Suit / Sleepwear / Underwear

Column Dress

Peasant Dress

Sundress

Sailor Dress

Bustier Dress

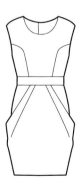

Tulip Dress

Kaftan Dress

Ball Gown

Traditionally a floor-length dress with a full skirt, ball gowns are the most formal social occasion attire for women and can be traced back to the Regency era. Constructed from luxurious textiles with delicate and exotic trimmings, it usually features a cut-off-the-shoulder décolleté neckline.

Petal Dress

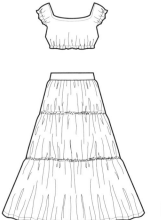

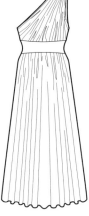

Qipao / Cheongsam

Gypsy Dress

One-shoulder Dress

75

APPAREL

Jacket / Coat / Shirt / Blouse / **Dress** / Vest / Sweater & Cardigan / Denim / Pants / Skirt / Jumpsuit / Suit / Sleepwear / Underwear

Trumpet Dress

Mermaid Dress

BACK VIEW

Backless Dress

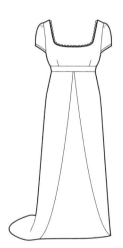

Regency Dress

Crinoline

Traditionally a stiffened petticoat or a stiff skirt-shaped steel structure, the crinoline was designed to be worn under the outer skirt to support its shape or to give it the defined silhouette desired. Nowadays, crinolines are usually worn as part of formal attire, such as wedding gowns or evening dresses, and the modernized version is usually constructed from multiple layers of rigid net or mesh, with flounces for skirt extension and occasionally with a plastic or nylon frame.

SIDE VIEW

Edwardian Dress

Bustle Dress

KNIT DRESSES

T-shirt Dress

Tank Dress

Zip-up Dress

Figure Skating Dress

Resembling regular street clothing before the 1920s, ice skating attire has since developed alongside the invention of stretch materials such as Lycra, and it has become a modern-day standard for figure skating fashion to be heavily embellished with crystals. When done perfectly, a skating dress synergizes artistry, comfort and movement, adding to the total experience of the ice skating performance by embodying the wearer's athletic prowess and cultural identity.

Wrapover Dress

Bandage Dress

Sweater Dress

2.6 **VEST**

A type of sleeveless upper-body garment that is usually worn by men beneath a coat or jacket, the vest (called a waistcoat in British English) is thought to be first popularized by King Charles II of England, who declared it a part of proper dress during the Restoration of the British monarchy. Its name originated from the French term *veste*, meaning 'jacket / sport coat,' the Italian word *vesta /veste*, meaning 'robe / gown' and the Latin word *vestis*.

79

APPAREL

Jacket / Coat / Shirt / Blouse / Dress / **Vest** / Sweater & Cardigan / Denim / Pants / Skirt / Jumpsuit / Suit / Sleepwear / Underwear

VEST DETAILS & MEASUREMENTS

X-shoulder Width

Armscye

Chest Circumference

Welt Pocket

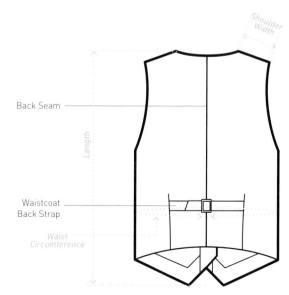

Shoulder Width

Back Seam

Length

Waistcoat Back Strap

Waist Circumference

Button Front Vest

Double-breasted Vest

Lapelled Vest

Waistcoat

Known as a 'waistcoat' in the UK and Commonwealth countries and a 'vest' in the US and Canada, it is typically worn as the third piece of a lounge suit in formal dress. Tailored with a full vertical front opening fastened with buttons or snaps, waistcoats are available in both single-breasted and double-breasted styles, with single-breasted ones being more common, though this is not definitive of the formality of the attire.

Short Vest

Long Vest

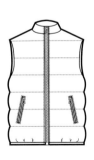

Down Vest /
Puffer Vest

81

APPAREL

Jacket / Coat / Shirt / Blouse / Dress / **Vest** / Sweater & Cardigan / Denim / Pants / Skirt / Jumpsuit / Suit / Sleepwear / Underwear

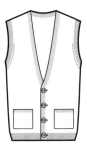

Cardigan Vest

Pullover Vest /
Sweater Vest

Tennis Vest

Hooded Vest

Safari Vest

Halter Vest / Piqué Vest

Made from textured woven piqué, the halter vest is a backless garment that is fully adjustable at the back of the neck and waist. It is a key component of white tie formal attire, which includes a tailcoat (dress coat), uncuffed formal trousers with braids on the outer legs, a white piqué vest (waistcoat), a white piqué front or plain starched wing collar dress shirt, black patent leather court shoes and accessories.

Punk Vest

Western Vest

Hippie Vest

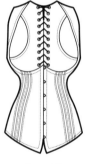

Corset Gilet

Bodice Vest

2.7 SWEATER AND CARDIGAN

A knitted item of clothing that generally covers the upper body and arms, a sweater (American English) was traditionally made from wool, while modern-day variations may be made from cotton, synthetic fibers or any combination of the aforementioned materials. It can either be a pullover or a cardigan. Pullovers are pulled on over the head, while cardigans are open at the front, usually with a button placket and sometimes with a zip closure.

CARDIGAN DETAILS & MEASUREMENTS

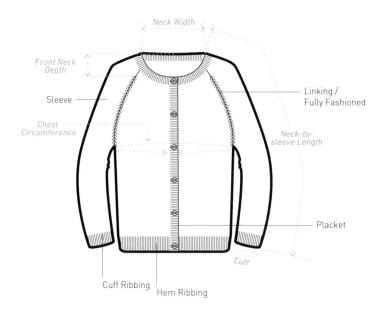

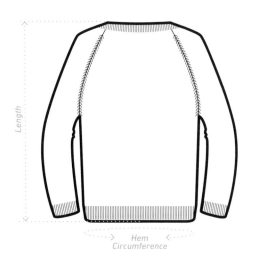

85

APPAREL

Jacket / Coat / Shirt / Blouse / Dress / Vest / **Sweater & Cardigan** / Denim / Pants / Skirt / Jumpsuit / Suit / Sleepwear / Underwear

SWEATERS

Crew Neck Sweater

Round Neck Sweater

V-neck Sweater

Henley Neck Sweater

Waisted Sweater

Cropped Sweater

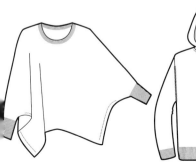

Batwing Sleeve Sweater

Hooded Sweater

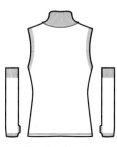

Sleeveless Sweater
with Gauntlets

Tunic Sweater

Polo Sweater

Zip-up Sweater

Cable Sweater /
Aran Sweater /
Fisherman Sweater

Lopapeysa /
Icelandic Sweater

The Icelandic sweater, also known as 'lopapeysa' in Icelandic language, is a type of sweater that originated from Iceland around or before the 1950s. During that period, imported clothing started to take over more traditional Icelandic garments, so locals began developing new ways to make use of the abundant supply of native wool. The patterns on lopapeysas are believed to be inspired by Greenlandic women's costumes and traditional textile patterns from Sweden, Turkey and South America.

Guernsey Sweater

87

APPAREL

Jacket / Coat / Shirt / Blouse / Dress / Vest / **Sweater & Cardigan** / Denim / Pants / Skirt / Jumpsuit / Suit / Sleepwear / Underwear

Fair Isle Sweater

Tyrolean Sweater

Lusekofte Sweater /
Norwegian Sweater

Cricket Sweater

Cowichan Sweater /
Mary Maxim Sweaters

Popular amongst local British Columbians and tourists,
Cowichan sweaters are fashioned using a form of knitting
called Cowichan knitting, developed by the Cowichan
natives of southeastern Vancouver Island in British
Columbia. Heavy-knit and distinctively patterned in a variety
of geometric, fish, whale, animal and bird motifs, Cowichan
sweaters are always handknit using thick, handspun, one-
ply natural-colored yarn in two to three colors, typically
black, grey and cream. The resulting garment is warm,
bulky and heavier than typical Scottish counterparts, such
as Fair Isle and Shetland garments, which are knit from
lightweight two-ply multi-color dyed yarn.

Ribbed Sweater

Argyle Sweater

Intarsia Sweater

Cable Knit Sweater

Turtleneck Sweater

Army Sweater

Poncho Sweater

Sailor Sweater

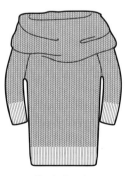

Chunky Sweater

Oversized Sweater

CARDIGANS

APPAREL

Jacket / Coat / Shirt / Blouse / Dress / Vest / **Sweater & Cardigan** / Denim / Pants / Skirt / Jumpsuit / Suit / Sleepwear / Underwear

Round Neck Cardigan

V-neck Cardigan

Zip-up Cardigan

Cropped Cardigan

Shawl Collar Cardigan

Wrap Cardigan

Faux Fur Shrug

Shrug / Bolero Cardigan

Ballet Cardigan

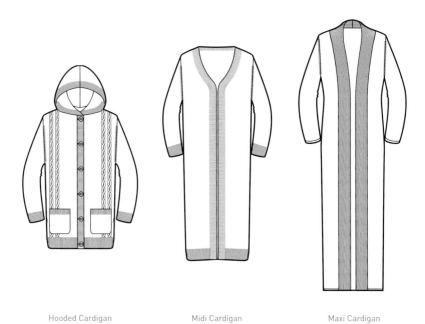

Hooded Cardigan   Midi Cardigan   Maxi Cardigan

2.8 DENIM AND JEANS

Known for its strong and durable qualities, denim is a cotton warp-faced twill fabric woven by passing the weft under two or more weft threads. Most indigo denim is customarily dyed only on the warp threads and uses undyed, plain white weft threads, thus displaying a visible blue color on the warp-dominant side of the fabric, while the reverse retains the white color of the weft threads as a result of warp-faced twill weaving. Jeans are generally defined as trousers made of denim or dungaree cloth.

DENIM JACKET DETAILS & MEASUREMENTS

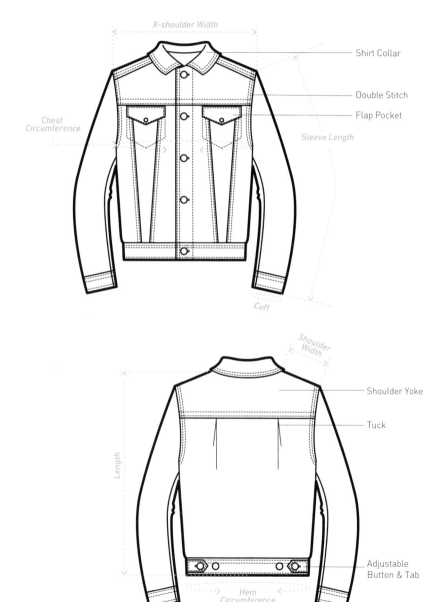

X-shoulder Width

Shirt Collar

Double Stitch

Flap Pocket

Chest Circumference

Sleeve Length

Cuff

Shoulder Width

Shoulder Yoke

Tuck

Length

Adjustable Button & Tab

Hem Circumference

93

APPAREL

Jacket / Coat / Shirt / Blouse / Dress / Vest / Sweater & Cardigan / **Denim** / Pants / Skirt / Jumpsuit / Suit / Sleepwear / Underwear

JEANS DETAILS & MEASUREMENTS

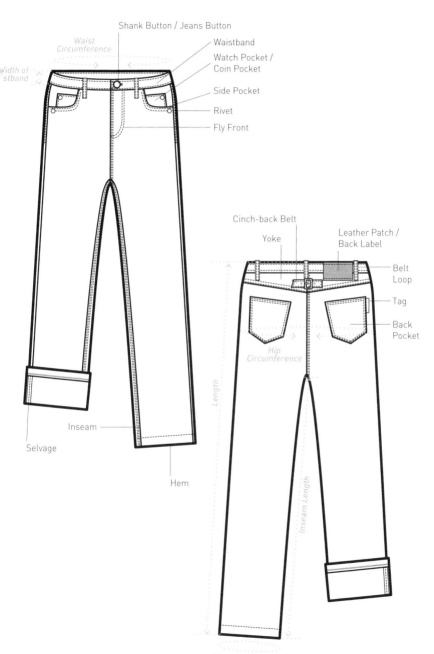

Shank Button / Jeans Button

Waist Circumference

Width of Waistband

Waistband

Watch Pocket / Coin Pocket

Side Pocket

Rivet

Fly Front

Cinch-back Belt

Yoke

Leather Patch / Back Label

Belt Loop

Tag

Back Pocket

Hip Circumference

Length

Inseam Length

Inseam

Selvage

Hem

Hem Circumference

DUNGAREES DETAILS & MEASUREMENTS

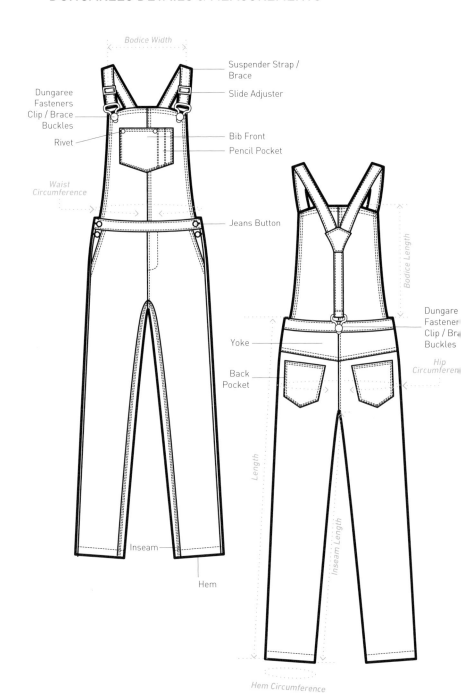

Bodice Width

Suspender Strap / Brace

Slide Adjuster

Dungaree Fasteners Clip / Brace Buckles

Rivet

Bib Front

Pencil Pocket

Waist Circumference

Jeans Button

Bodice Length

Dungaree Fastener Clip / Brace Buckles

Hip Circumference

Yoke

Back Pocket

Length

Inseam Length

Inseam

Hem

Hem Circumference

APPAREL

Jacket / Coat / Shirt / Blouse / Dress / Vest / Sweater & Cardigan / **Denim** / Pants / Skirt / Jumpsuit / Suit / Sleepwear / Underwear

Standard Denim Jacket

Stormrider Jacket

Sherpa-lined Denim Jacket

Cropped Denim Jacket

Denim Shirt

Denim Bustier

Denim Corset

Denim Skirt

Denim Shorts

Straight Jeans

In 1871, Jacob Davis invented blue jeans and jointly patented the design with Levi Strauss in 1873. Levi Strauss & Co. also trademarked the orange thread used for stitching their jeans, which serves as a brand-distinctive feature as well as matching the color of the copper rivets. Originally designed for cowboys and miners in the 1950s, jeans have become a fashion staple nowadays, with approximately 450 million pairs sold every year in the United States alone.

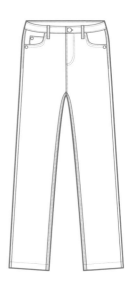

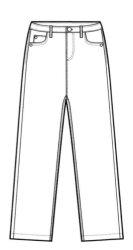

Skinny Jeans   Tapered Jeans   Baggy Jeans

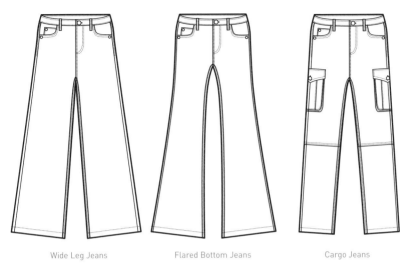

Wide Leg Jeans

Flared Bottom Jeans

Cargo Jeans

Button Fly Jeans

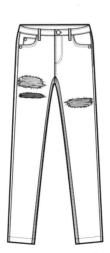

Ripped Jeans

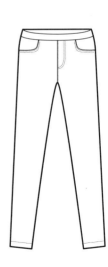

Jeggings

jeggings are usually made of a spandex-blend denim or are a type of leggings made to look like denim jeans with fake pockets and belt fly

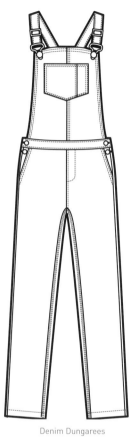

Denim Dungarees

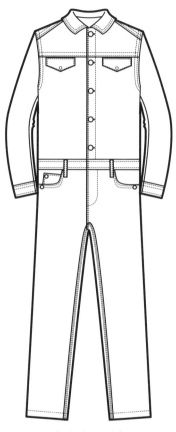

Denim Jumpsuit /
Denim Overalls

2.9 PANTS

Pants (called trousers in British English) are a type of garment which covers the legs separately from the waist to the ankles. The variation in which the pants legs only reach above, below or at knee length is called shorts. In the majority of Western society, pants have existed since ancient times and were worn throughout the Medieval Age, subsequently becoming the most common type of lower-body clothing for men in the modern era. Trousers have been increasingly worn by females since the mid-20th century.

PANTS DETAILS & MEASUREMENTS

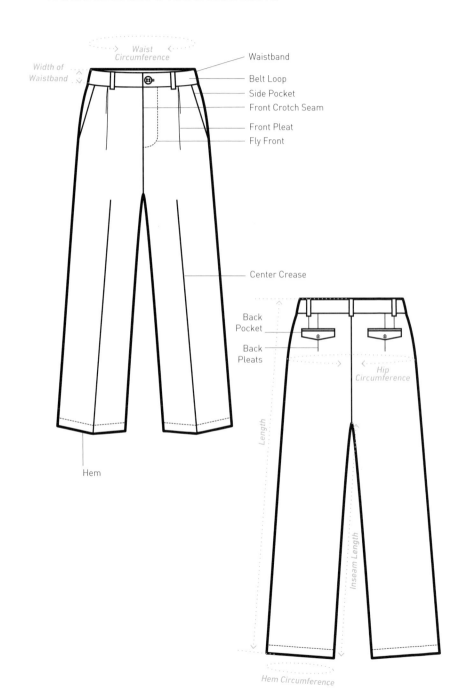

Waist Circumference

Width of Waistband

Waistband

Belt Loop

Side Pocket

Front Crotch Seam

Front Pleat

Fly Front

Center Crease

Back Pocket

Back Pleats

Hip Circumference

Length

Inseam Length

Hem

Hem Circumference

APPAREL

Jacket / Coat / Shirt / Blouse / Dress / Vest / Sweater & Cardigan / Denim / **Pants** / Skirt / Jumpsuit / Suit / Sleepwear / Underwear

TYPES OF PANTS

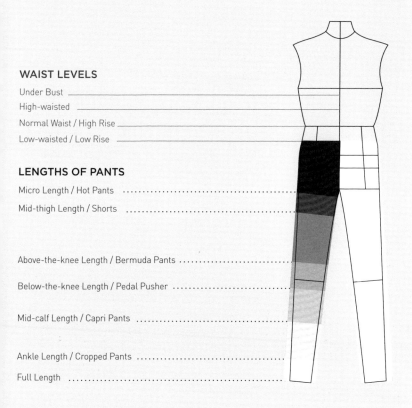

WAIST LEVELS

Under Bust
High-waisted
Normal Waist / High Rise
Low-waisted / Low Rise

LENGTHS OF PANTS

Micro Length / Hot Pants
Mid-thigh Length / Shorts

Above-the-knee Length / Bermuda Pants
Below-the-knee Length / Pedal Pusher

Mid-calf Length / Capri Pants

Ankle Length / Cropped Pants
Full Length

SILHOUETTES OF PANTS
(SIDE VIEW)

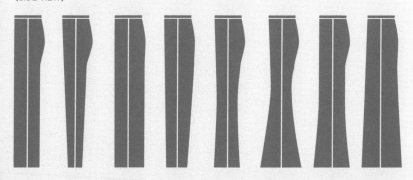

Straight   Slim Fit   Baggy   Peg Top   Boot Cut   Bell Bottom   Flare   Wide Leg

WOVEN PANTS

Micro Shorts /
Hot Pants

Bloomers

Tap Pants

Shorts

Bermuda Shorts /
Dress Shorts

Also known as dress shorts or walking shorts, Bermuda
shorts are a type of short pants worn by both males and
females as part of a semi-casual outfit. The name is derived
from the Bermudas, a British Overseas Territory where the
shorts became popular and were considered appropriate
business attire when made from suiting materials and
paired with a dress shirt, tie, blazer and knee-length socks.

Surfboard Pants /
Boardshorts

Cargo Shorts

Preppy Shorts

Baggy Bermudas

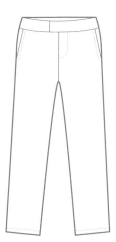

Capri Pants

With legs cropped at mid-calf length, Capri pants are a favorite style worn in warm weather. First introduced in 1948 by European fashion designer Sonja de Lennart, Capri pants were named after the Italian Isle of Capri, where they became highly sought after in the late 1950s to early 60s. American actress Grace Kelly helped popularize the style as she was one of the first movie stars to wear them on the island.

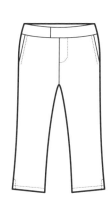

Pedal Pusher Pants

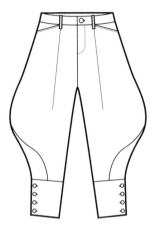

Riding Breeches

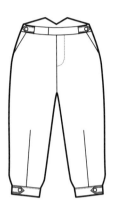

Plus Fours

Sarouel Pants

Also known as the sirwals, sarouel pants are worn in Muslim communities and also some places in India. They were originally introduced from Persia to Muslim countries.

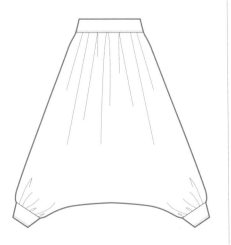

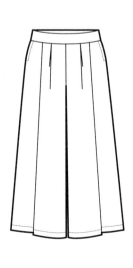

Gaucho Pants

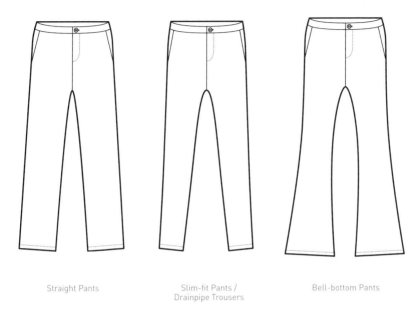

Straight Pants

Slim-fit Pants /
Drainpipe Trousers

Bell-bottom Pants

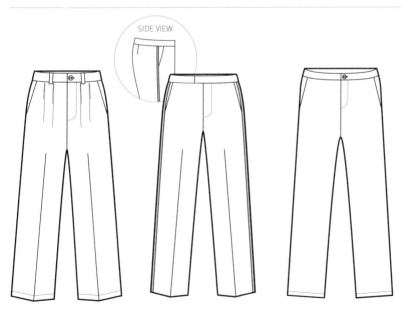

SIDE VIEW

Tailored Pants

Tuxedo Pants

Flat Front Pants

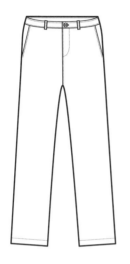

Chinos

made from chino cloth

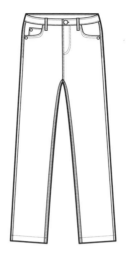

Jeans

Oxford Bags

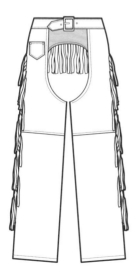

Chaps / Cowboy Pants

seperate pants are worn inside

Zouave Pants

Harem Pants

Palazzo Pants

A type of long women's pants cut with loose and dramatically wide legs that flare out from the waist to resemble a skirt, Palazzo pants are usually made from light, flowing and breathable fabrics, making them a popular and flattering choice in hot summer climates.

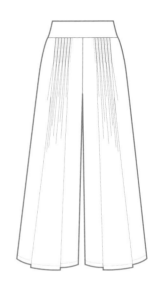

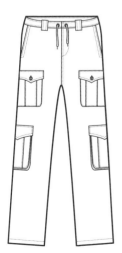

Cargo Pants

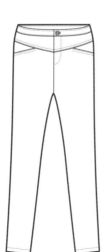

Yoked Pants

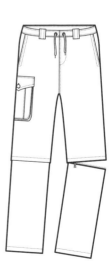

Zip-off Convertible Pants

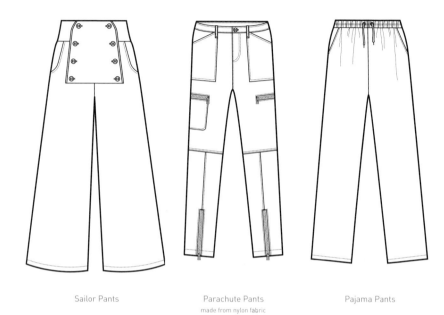

Sailor Pants

Parachute Pants
made from nylon fabric

Pajama Pants

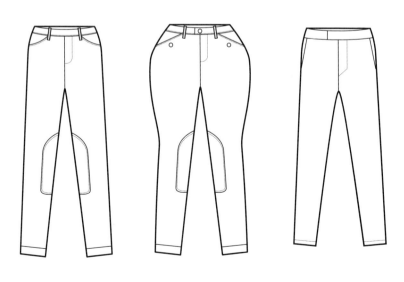

Kentucky Jodhpurs

Classic Jodhpurs

Cigarette Pants

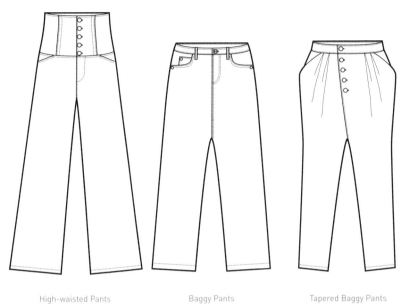

High-waisted Pants

Baggy Pants

Tapered Baggy Pants

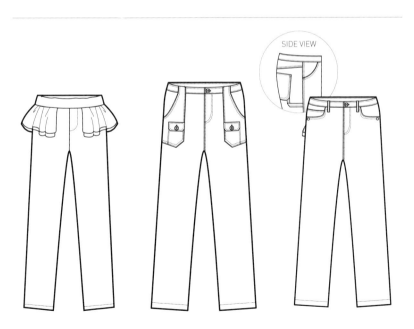

SIDE VIEW

Peplum Pants

Bush Pants

Carpenter Pants

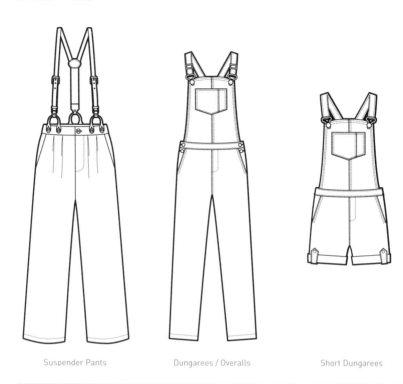

Suspender Pants

Dungarees / Overalls

Short Dungarees

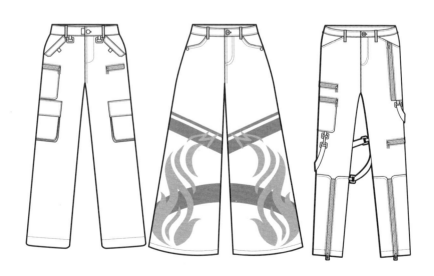

Ski Pants

Phat Pants
decorated with UV reflective tape
to add a glowing effect

Bondage Pants

KNIT PANTS

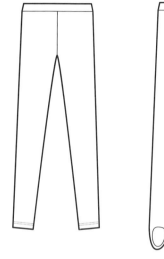

Leggings

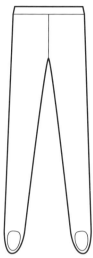

Stirrup Pants

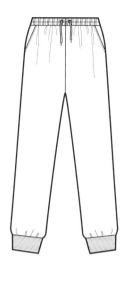

Sweatpants

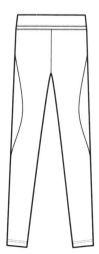

Yoga Pants

Cycling Pants

2.10 **SKIRT**

———

A skirt is generally defined as a tube- or cone-shaped piece of clothing from the waist or hips down, covering all or portions of the legs. The cutting of skirts varies in terms of complexity, with the simplest types consisting of only a single piece of draped fabric, such as pareos. Skirts are usually tailored to fit at the waist or hips and flare towards the hem, creating a full silhouette by inserting darts, pleats, godets or panels. Variations of skirts exist in many different cultures and are worn by both genders, such as sarongs, lungis and kangas worn by women in South and Southeastern Asia, and kilts worn by men in Scotland and Ireland.

113

APPAREL

Jacket / Coat / Shirt / Blouse / Dress / Vest / Sweater & Cardigan / Denim / Pants / Skirt / Jumpsuit / Suit / Sleepwear / Underwear

SKIRT DETAILS & MEASUREMENTS

Waistband

Waist Circumference

Width of Waistband

Waist Dart

Hem Circumference

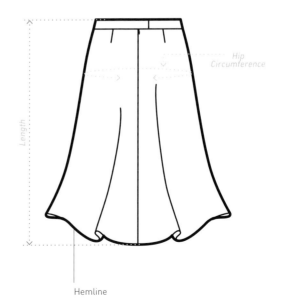

Length

Hip Circumference

Hemline

LENGTHS AND FULLNESS OF SKIRT

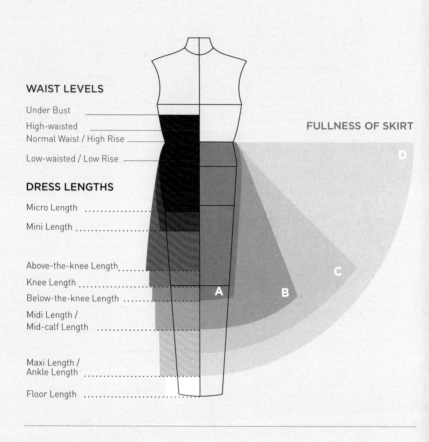

WAIST LEVELS

Under Bust

High-waisted

Normal Waist / High Rise

Low-waisted / Low Rise

DRESS LENGTHS

Micro Length

Mini Length

Above-the-knee Length

Knee Length

Below-the-knee Length

Midi Length /
Mid-calf Length

Maxi Length /
Ankle Length

Floor Length

FULLNESS OF SKIRT

A

B

C

D

FULLNESS OF SKIRT

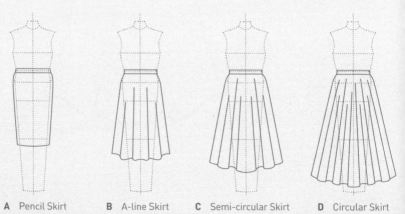

A Pencil Skirt **B** A-line Skirt **C** Semi-circular Skirt **D** Circular Skirt

APPAREL

Jacket / Coat / Shirt / Blouse / Dress / Vest / Sweater & Cardigan / Denim / Pants / **Skirt** / Jumpsuit / Suit / Sleepwear / Underwear

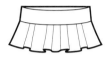

Micro Skirt

Leather Skirt

Denim Skirt

Balloon Skirt

Mini Skirt

Mini skirts are distinguished by their high hemlines, which always hit well above the knees and usually at mid-thigh length. The style peaked in popularity during the Swinging Sixties of London but remains fashionable till today. It is generally acknowledged that André Courrèges and Mary Quant invented the skirt at approximately the same time. Quant thought of the mini skirts as practical and liberating, letting women run freely for the bus.

Culotte Short Skirt

FRONT VIEW

BACK VIEW

Skort

Rah-rah Skirt

Sarong Skirt /
Pareo Skirt

Peplum Skirt

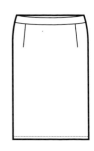

Sheath Skirt

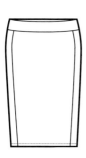

Pencil Skirt /
Tapered Skirt

Dirndl Skirt

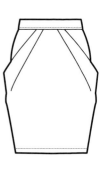

Peg-top Skirt

117

APPAREL

Jacket / Coat / Shirt / Blouse / Dress / Vest / Sweater & Cardigan / Denim / Pants / **Skirt** / Jumpsuit / Suit / Sleepwear / Underwear

A-line Skirt

The term 'A-line skirt' was first introduced by
French couturier Christian Dior as the label
of one of his three collections for Spring/
Summer 1955. Fitted at the hips, usually with
seams and/or darts, and widening towards
the hem, an A-line skirt is defined by a
silhouette that resembles the shape of the
capital letter A. It is free from visible ease-
enhancing features such as pleats, vents or
slits to maintain a clean and streamlined
structure.

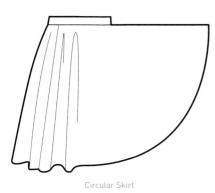

Circular Skirt

Flared Skirt / Skater Skirt

Full Skirt

Tutu Skirt

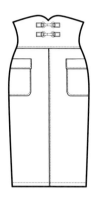

High-waisted Skirt

Yoke Skirt

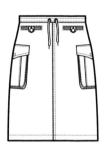

Cargo Skirt

Ruffle Skirt

Button-down Skirt

Bell Skirt

Draped Skirt

Apron Skirt

Wrap Skirt

119

APPAREL

Jacket / Coat / Shirt / Blouse / Dress / Vest / Sweater & Cardigan / Denim / Pants / **Skirt** / Jumpsuit / Suit / Sleepwear / Underwear

Mini Crinoline Skirt

Kilt

Ballerina Skirt

Handkerchief Skirt

Sunray Pleat Skirt

Kick Pleat Skirt /
Inverted Pleat Skirt

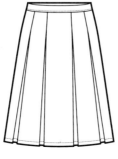

Box Pleat Skirt

Side Pleat Skirt /
Knife Pleat Skirt

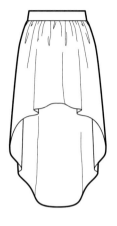

High-low Skirt

Cascade Skirt

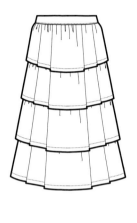

Tiered Skirt

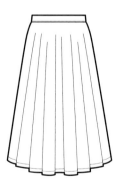

Midi Skirt

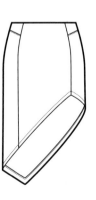

Asymmetric Skirt

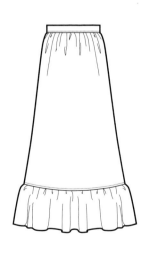

Prairie Skirt

121

APPAREL

Jacket / Coat / Shirt / Blouse / Dress / Vest / Sweater & Cardigan / Denim / Pants / Skirt / Jumpsuit / Suit / Sleepwear / Underwear

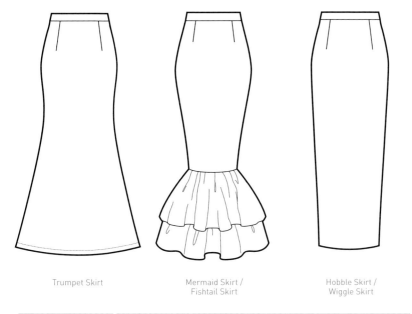

Trumpet Skirt

Mermaid Skirt /
Fishtail Skirt

Hobble Skirt /
Wiggle Skirt

Slit Skirt

Gypsy Skirt

Eight-gore Skirt

Petticoat Skirt for Gown

A petticoat generally refers to any
separate skirt or skirt-like undergarment
worn with a gown, bedgown, bodice or
jacket, with the purpose of keeping
warm or giving the outer skirt or dress
the defined shape desired. Owing to
modern-day trends for extravagant
weddings and elaborate
bridalwear, petticoats are now
commonly worn to support
the full-skirted silhouette of
wedding gowns and to retain
their intended shapes.

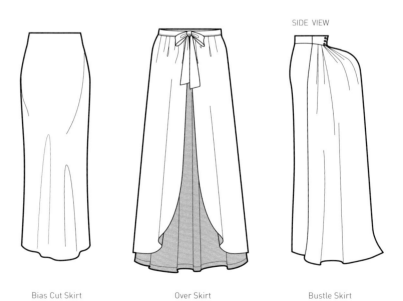

Bias Cut Skirt

Over Skirt

SIDE VIEW

Bustle Skirt

Maxi Skirt

Poodle Skirt

Grass Skirt /
Hula Skirt

Flamenco Skirt

Part of the costume known as 'traje de
flamenca' (flamenco outfit) worn by female
performers of the Flamenco, a type of
Spanish folk music and dance from the
Andalusia region in southern Spain,
a flamenco skirt is an ankle-length
skirt embellished with ruffles.

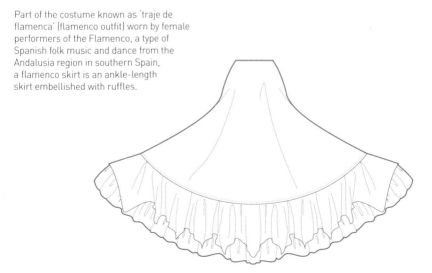

2.11 JUMPSUIT AND OVERALLS

Originally referring to the functional one-piece clothing worn by skydivers and parachuters, the term 'jumpsuit' has nowadays become broadly adapted to describe any all-in-one garment with a conjoined bodice and pants, with or without sleeves.

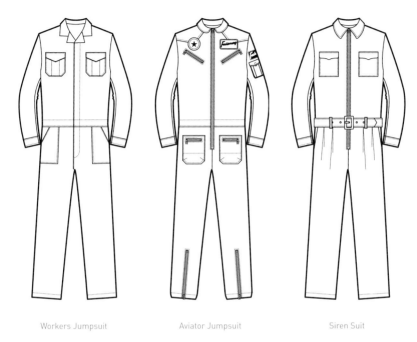

Workers Jumpsuit

Aviator Jumpsuit

Siren Suit

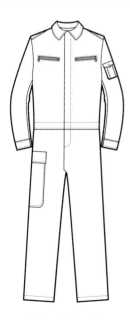

Boilersuit / Coveralls

Camisole Jumpsuit

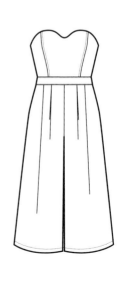

Culotte Jumpsuit

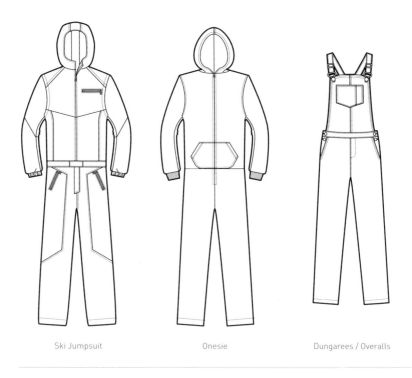

Ski Jumpsuit

Onesie

Dungarees / Overalls

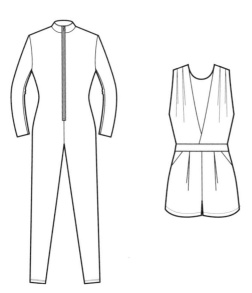

Catsuit

Playsuit / Rompers

2.12 **SUIT**

A standardized set of garments comprising multiple components (jacket, trousers and vest) made of the same fabric and designed to be worn together and 'follow' each other, suits derive their name from the French word *suite*, which means 'following', and from a Late Latin derivative of the Latin verb *sequor*, meaning 'I follow'. Brooks Brothers is generally acknowledged for creating the first 'ready-to-wear' suit, which could be purchased already manufactured and sized, and ready for tailoring. Haggar Company pioneered the concept of suit separates in the USA, introducing the idea of individually sold jackets and pants which remains popular on the market today.

SUIT CLASSIFICATION

A suit is a set of garments made from the same fabric. There are four main types of suits:

/ **Two-piece Suit**
/ **Three-piece Suit**
/ **Single-breasted Suit**
/ **Double-breasted Suit**

Suits are commonly sold in four ways nowadays:

/ **Bespoke**
custom-made by the tailor from a pattern created from the customer's measurements

/ **Made-to-measure**
a pre-made pattern is modified to fit the customer

/ **Ready-to-wear**
produced in standard sizes

/ **Suit Separates**
jacket and pants are sold separately to allow the customer to choose the size that is best for them

Three–piece Suit

A modern spin on the classic men's suit, a three-piece suit includes a vest in addition to the jacket and trousers. Also known as a 'vested suit', the three-piece suit is in fact more traditional than its more common two-piece counterpart, as it was the established standard prior to the 1960s. With three components, the vested suit greatly enhances versatility and wearability, as it allows the wearer the flexibility of either wearing all three pieces together or just two pieces, such as the jacket and trousers without the vest, or alternatively only the trousers with the vest while indoors.

SUITS FOR MEN

APPAREL

Jacket / Coat / Shirt / Blouse / Dress / Vest / Sweater & Cardigan / Denim / Pants / Skirt / Jumpsuit / **Suit** / Sleepwear / Underwear

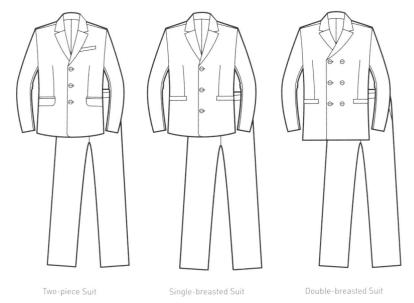

Two-piece Suit

Single-breasted Suit

Double-breasted Suit

Separates

Cardigan Suit

Mao Suit / Tunic Suit

SUITS FOR WOMEN

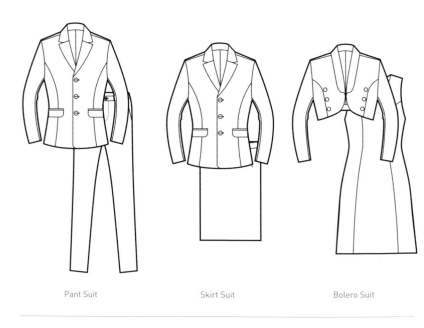

Pant Suit   Skirt Suit   Bolero Suit

Culotte Suit   Chanel-style Suit

2.13 SLEEPWEAR AND NIGHTWEAR

Nightwear is a type of garment intended to be worn for sleeping, the style of which may vary depending on the season. Warmer styles may be worn in colder months and vice versa.

Slip Dress

Nightgown

Also called a nightie or nightdress, a nightgown is a loose-fitting item of nightwear, worn almost only by women nowadays. It can be made of cotton, silk or nylon, sometimes embellished with lace appliqué or embroidery at the bodice and hem.

Babydoll

Negligee

made of soft and sheer fabric

Nightshirt

APPAREL

Jacket / Coat / Shirt / Blouse / Dress / Vest / Sweater & Cardigan / Denim / Pants / Skirt / Jumpsuit / Suit / **Sleepwear** / Underwear

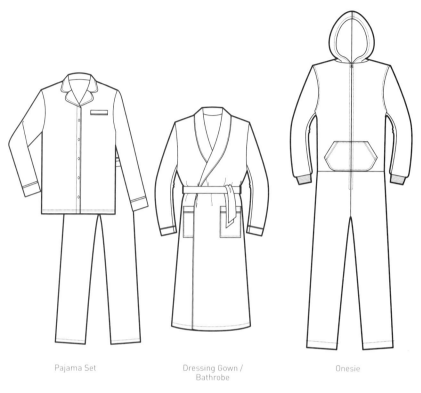

Pajama Set

Dressing Gown /
Bathrobe

Onesie

Kimono Nightwear

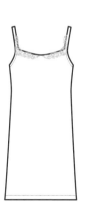

Chemise

Camisole Pajama Set

2.14 UNDERWEAR

———

Worn beneath outer clothing and usually directly touching the skin, underwear includes both upper and lower body garments and may consist of one or more layers. A main purpose of underwear is to keep outer garments from direct contact with the body, hence preventing them from being damaged and soiled by bodily substances, as well as lessening their abrasion and friction against the skin. It also helps shape, conceal and support parts of the body.

BRASSIERE DETAILS & MEASUREMENTS

APPAREL

Jacket / Coat / Shirt / Blouse / Dress / Vest / Sweater & Cardigan / Denim / Pants / Skirt / Jumpsuit / Suit / Sleepwear / **Underwear**

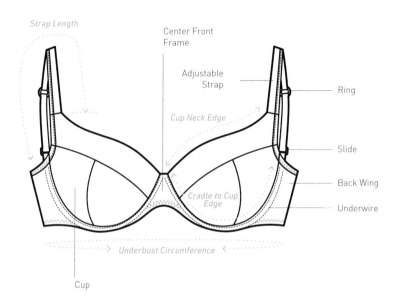

Strap Length

Center Front
Frame

Adjustable
Strap

Ring

Cup Neck Edge

Slide

Back Wing

Cradle to Cup Edge

Underwire

Underbust Circumference

Cup

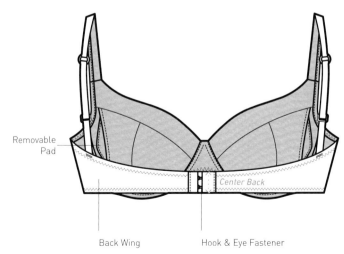

Removable
Pad

Center Back

Back Wing

Hook & Eye Fastener

MEN'S BRIEF DETAILS & MEASUREMENTS

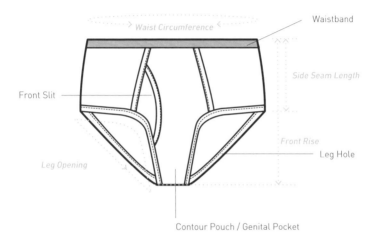

Waistband

Waist Circumference

Side Seam Length

Front Slit

Front Rise

Leg Hole

Leg Opening

Contour Pouch / Genital Pocket

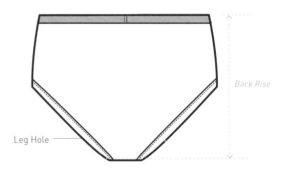

Back Rise

Leg Hole

EVOLUTION OF BRAS / BRASSIERES

APPAREL

Jacket / Coat / Shirt / Blouse / Dress / Vest / Sweater & Cardigan / Denim / Pants / Skirt / Jumpsuit / Suit / Sleepwear / Underwear

Designed to push the breasts upward, corsets dominated the undergarment trend amongst wealthier women in the Western world starting from the 16th century. During the late 19th century, clothing designers started experimenting with ways to modernize corsets, such as segmenting them into various parts: girdle-like devices for restricting the abdomen, and breast-suspenders supported by the shoulder.

The first modern brassiere was patented in 1889 by German inventor Christine Hardt. In 1912, the first brassiere specifically developed for mass production was introduced by Sigmund Lindauer, who came from a family of corset makers from Stuttgart-Bad Cannstatt, Germany. Lindauer subsequently patented his design in 1913, and it was put into mass production by Mechanische Trikotweberei Ludwig Maier und Cie. in Germany. In 1914, Mary Phelps Jacob was granted a patent in the United States for her 'backless brassiere', the first brassiere design that has been recognized as the foundation of modern-day bras.

Due to the shortage of metal during World War I, corsets were gradually replaced by brassieres, which were worn by most fashion-conscious women in Europe and North America by the time the war ended. The brassiere trend subsequently spread to the rest of the world and became widely adopted by women in Latin America, Asia and Africa.

BRAS

Balconette

First introduced in about 1938 in the United States and becoming mainstream in the 1950s, the balconette bra is designed to lift the breasts and enhance their appearance with its balcony-like shape, from which it got its name 'balconette', literally meaning 'little balcony'. A balconette cup always cut horizontally just above the bust line.

Full Support Bra

Full Cup Bra

Plunge Bra

Soft Cup Bra

Padded Bra /
Push-up Bra

Contour Bra /
Molded Cup Bra

Shelf Bra /
Open Cup Bra

Underwire Bra

Front Closure Bra

139

APPAREL

Jacket / Coat / Shirt / Blouse / Dress / Vest / Sweater & Cardigan / Denim / Pants / Skirt / Jumpsuit / Suit / Sleepwear / Underwear

Demi Cup Bra /
Half Cup Bra

Demi cup bras cover half to three quarters of the breasts and can uplift the breasts as well as create cleavage. The industry generally cuts a demi cup to 1" above the nipple point.

Longline Bra

Maternity Bra

Bullet Bra

Strapless Bra

Racerback Bra

Convertible Bra

Backless Bra

Posture Bra

Triangle Bra

Sheer Bra

Bralette

Peephole Bra

Sleep Bra

Training Bra

Tube Bra

Athletic Bra /
Sports Bra

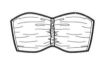

Bandeau

Adhesive Bra /
Nude Bra

PANTIES / KNICKERS

Classic Briefs

High-cut Briefs

Boyleg Briefs /
Boyshorts / Girl Boxers

PANTIES / KNICKERS (CONT'D)

APPAREL

Jacket / Coat / Shirt / Blouse / Dress / Vest / Sweater & Cardigan / Denim / Pants / Skirt / Jumpsuit / Suit / Sleepwear / **Underwear**

Control Briefs

BACK VIEW

G-string

First seen in Earl Carroll's theater productions during the Jazz Age, the G-string was part of the costumes worn by showgirls. The letter 'G' is believed to stand for 'groin' as deemed by linguist Robert Hendrickson. It may be worn as underwear instead of panties to avoid showing a visible panty line.

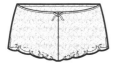

French Knickers

Hipsters

Bikinis

String Bikinis

Tangas

BACK VIEW

Cheeky Thongs

BACK VIEW   3/4 VIEW

C-string

BACK VIEW

V-string

BACK VIEW

T-back

CORSETRY

Hourglass Corset

Waist Cincher

Boned and back-laced, a waist cincher is a
type of belt intended to make the wearer's
waist physically smaller or to create the
impression of such. It was first made popular
around 1947, when Christian Dior introduced
it with the brand's iconic style the 'New Look'.
Only around 6 to 7 inches, it differs from a
historical Victorian corset mainly with its
narrower length.

Bustier

Torsolette / Basque

Corselet / Corselette /
Merry Widow

Panty Girdle

Open Bottom Girdle

Pointed Cincher

SLIPS

Slip Dress

Teddy

Teddiette

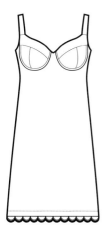

Bra Slip

Chemise

Meaning 'shirt' in French, chemises were traditionally worn as smock shirts by both men and women. Nowadays, they generally mean sleeveless, loose-fitting undergarments or lingerie that are not cinched at the waist.

OTHER WOMEN'S UNDERWEAR

Bodysuit

Garter Briefs

Suspender Belt /
Garter Belt

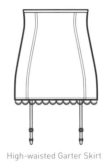

High-waisted Garter Skirt

Garter

MEN'S UNDERPANTS

Y-front Briefs

Narrow Front Briefs

Tanga

BACK VIEW

Jock Strap

Thong

Unilateral Thong

MEN'S UNDERPANTS (CONT'D)

Boxer Briefs

A newer, hybrid form of men's undergarment, boxer briefs are cut with longer legs like boxer shorts, but offer a tighter fit like briefs. They were first introduced by John Varvatos, head of menswear design at Calvin Klein in 1990.

Trunks

Boxer Shorts

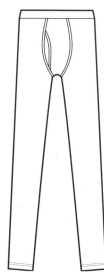

Long Johns

THE DETAIL IS AS IMPORTANT AS THE ESSENTIAL IS. WHEN IT IS INADEQUATE, IT DESTROYS THE WHOLE OUTFIT.

/ CHRISTIAN DIOR

03 DETAIL

———

NECKLINE / COLLAR / LAPEL / SLEEVE / CUFF / OPENING / POCKET / JACKET DETAIL / SHIRT DETAIL / PANTS DETAIL / JEANS DETAIL

3.1 **NECKLINE**

Halterneck

A halterneck garment features a single strap or material which runs around the wearer's neck. One of the most famous dresses in history is the white halterneck dress worn by Marilyn Monroe in the 1955 movie, *The Seven Year Itch*.

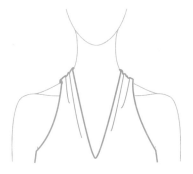

Round

V-neckline

Oval

U-neckline

Horseshoe

Sweetheart

Boat / Bateau

Scoop

Square

Plunge

Trapeze

V-shaped Crew

149

DETAIL

Neckline / Collar / Lapel / Sleeve / Cuff / Opening / Pocket / Jacket Detail / Shirt Detail / Pants Detail / Jeans Detail

Asymmetric

High / Bottle

Turtleneck

Diamond

Keyhole

Heart-shaped

Scalloped

Petal

Ballerina

Wrapped

Surplice

Strapless

Florentine

Notched

Slashed

Suit

Off-the-shoulder

Funnel

Zigzag

One-shoulder

Camisole

Crew

Henley

Gathered

Tucked

Cowl

Halterneck

Drawstring

3.2 **COLLAR**

Peter Pan Collar

The Peter Pan collar is named after the costume of Maude Adam who starred as Peter Pan in the 1905 play, Peter and Wendy. It has been mainly associated with children's wear since the 1920s.

Regular

Spread

Pointed / Barrymore

Long Button-down

Short Button-down

Tab

Full Cutaway

Mitered

Round

Eton

Edwardian

Wing

Narrow

Imperial

Stand-away

Banded / Stand

Mandarin

Clerical

Flat

Open

Peter Pan

Low

Horseshoe

Pinned

Puritan

Asymmetric

Notched

Chelsea

Shawl

Double

Sailor / Middy

Loop

Flat Knit / Polo

Johnny

Pussy Bow

Poet

Jabot

Medici

Pierrot

Ruff Collar

3.3 **LAPEL**

Notched Lapel

A lapel which is sewn to the collar at an angle and creates a stepped effect is called a notched lapel. Notched lapels are always found on single-breasted suit jackets.

Notched

Semi-notched

Fish Mouth

Peaked / Pointed

Semi-peaked

Round Collar Peak

Round Peak

Clover

Half Clover

Shawl

Notched Shawl

Tab

Framed

open

Balmacaan

Ulster

Chesterfield

Napoleon

L-shaped

T-shaped

153

DETAIL

Neckline / Collar / **Lapel** / **Sleeve** / Cuff / Opening / Pocket / Jacket Detail / Shirt Detail / Pants Detail / Jeans Detail

3.4 **SLEEVE**

Bouffant Sleeve

A bouffant sleeve is a larger and fuller version of the puff sleeve. It is usually gathered at the cuff and the shoulder.

Set-in

Raglan

Semi-raglan

Epaulet

Yoke

Cap

Tulip

Tucked

Flare

Angel

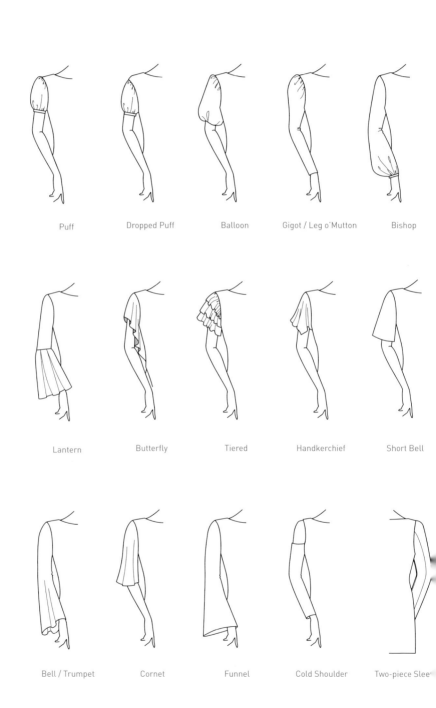

Puff

Dropped Puff

Balloon

Gigot / Leg o'Mutton

Bishop

Lantern

Butterfly

Tiered

Handkerchief

Short Bell

Bell / Trumpet

Cornet

Funnel

Cold Shoulder

Two-piece Slee

155

DETAIL

Neckline / Collar / Lapel / **Sleeve** / Cuff / Opening / Pocket / Jacket Detail / Shirt Detail / Pants Detail / Jeans Detail

Slashed

Crescent

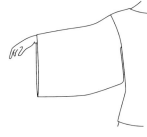

Traditional Kimono
Sleeve

Pagoda

Paned

Virago

Batwing

Poet

Juliet

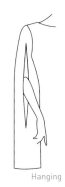

Hanging

Dolman

3.5 **CUFF**

Cuff

The extra layer of fabric which is attached to the end of a sleeve is called a cuff. It is always divided along one edge, allowing enough room for the hand to pass through, and fitting around the wrist after fastening, usually with one or more buttons.

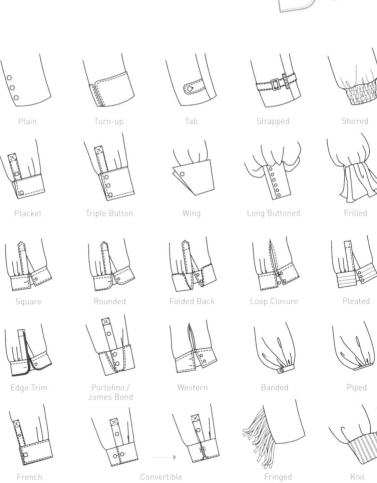

Plain	Turn-up	Tab	Strapped	Shirred
Placket	Triple Button	Wing	Long Buttoned	Frilled
Square	Rounded	Folded Back	Loop Closure	Pleated
Edge Trim	Portofino / James Bond	Western	Banded	Piped
French for cufflinks	Convertible		Fringed	Knit

157

DETAIL

Neckline / Collar / Lapel / Sleeve / Cuff / Opening / Pocket / Jacket Detail / Shirt Detail / Pants Detail / Jeans Detail

3.6 **OPENING**

Opening

It can be dated back to over a century ago when the buttons on men's and women's clothing were on different sides. It is believed that men always dressed themselves, so having buttons on the right hand side would be suitable for most men (who are right-handed). Women who could afford fancy clothing with buttons would rely on maids to help them get dressed. Maids would prefer to have buttons on their own right hand side (which is on the left side of the clothing).

Men's Jacket
Opening

Women's Jacket
Opening

Single-breasted

Double-breasted

Slashed

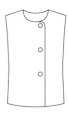

Button

Zipper /
Slide Fastener

Placket

Fly Front

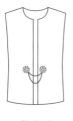

Chained

Asymmetric

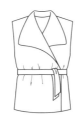

Wrap

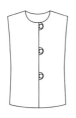

Button & Loop

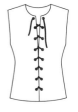

Lacing

Buckle

Chinese Button

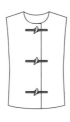

Toggle

3.7 **POCKET**

POCKET TYPES

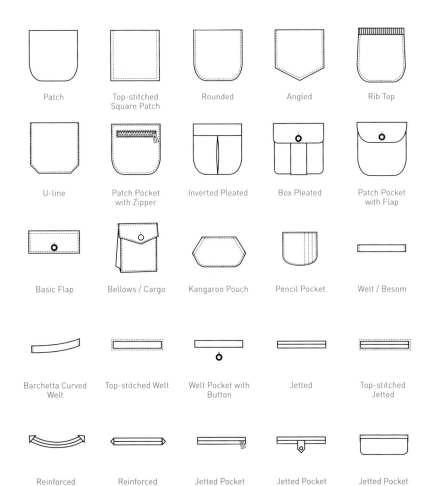

Patch

Top-stitched
Square Patch

Rounded

Angled

Rib Top

U-line

Patch Pocket
with Zipper

Inverted Pleated

Box Pleated

Patch Pocket
with Flap

Basic Flap

Bellows / Cargo

Kangaroo Pouch

Pencil Pocket

Welt / Besom

Barchetta Curved
Welt

Top-stitched Welt

Welt Pocket with
Button

Jetted

Top-stitched
Jetted

Reinforced
Western Jetted

Reinforced
Jetted

Jetted Pocket
with Zipper

Jetted Pocket
with Tab

Jetted Pocket
with Flap

159

DETAIL

Neckline / Collar / Lapel / Sleeve / Cuff / Opening / **Pocket** / Jacket Detail / Shirt Detail / Pants Detail / Jeans Detail

POCKETS ON JACKETS

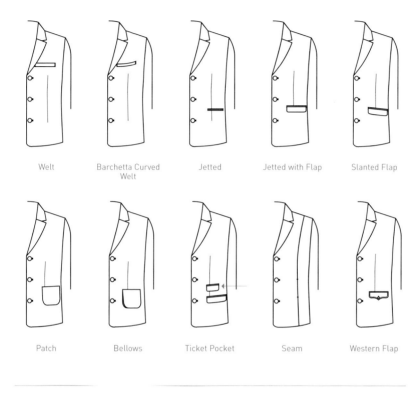

Welt

Barchetta Curved Welt

Jetted

Jetted with Flap

Slanted Flap

Patch

Bellows

Ticket Pocket

Seam

Western Flap

POCKETS ON PANTS

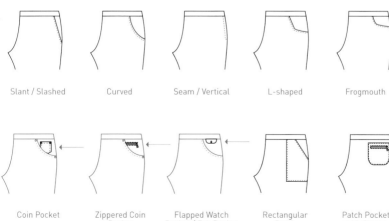

Slant / Slashed

Curved

Seam / Vertical

L-shaped

Frogmouth

Coin Pocket

Zippered Coin Pocket

Flapped Watch Pocket / Fob Pocket

Rectangular Patch

Patch Pocket with Zipper

3.8 JACKET DETAIL

SHOULDER LINES

Straight

Natural

Dropped

Wide

Square

Roped
has slightly more padding
than a natural shoulder

Concave /
Pagoda

Arched

Neapolitan /
Spalla /
Manica Camicia

Extended

BACK DART AND SEAM

Center Back
Seam

Princess Seam

Armhole
Princess Seam

Waist Dart

Armhole Dart

Shoulder Dart

FRONT CUT

Rounded Cut

Regular Cut

Square Cut

Cutaway

3.9 **SHIRT DETAIL**

DETAIL

Neckline / Collar / Lapel / Sleeve / Cuff / Opening / Pocket / **Jacket Detail** / **Shirt Detail** / Pants Detail / Jeans Detail

FRONT YOKES

| Horizontal | Diagonal | Western | Scalloped | Inverted Pleat | Snap Down |

BACK YOKES

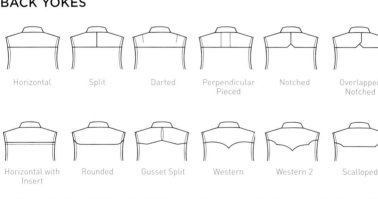

| Horizontal | Split | Darted | Perpendicular Pieced | Notched | Overlapped Notched |

| Horizontal with Insert | Rounded | Gusset Split | Western | Western 2 | Scalloped |

HEMS

| Straight | Shirt Hem | Shirttail Hem | Banded | Baseball |

| Gathered | Tie | Flare | Peplum | High-low |

3.10   PANTS DETAIL

PANTS FRONT

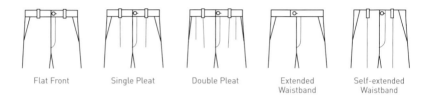

Flat Front   Single Pleat   Double Pleat   Extended Waistband   Self-extended Waistband

SIDE POCKETS

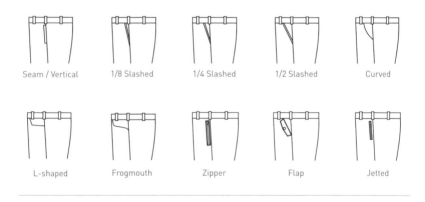

Seam / Vertical   1/8 Slashed   1/4 Slashed   1/2 Slashed   Curved

L-shaped   Frogmouth   Zipper   Flap   Jetted

BELT LOOPS

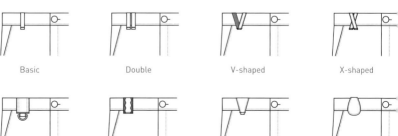

Basic   Double   V-shaped   X-shaped

Wide with D-Ring   Leather-trimmed Wide Loop   Inverted Trapezoid   Horseshoe

3.11 JEANS DETAIL

3 pockets on the front

2 pockets at the back

Five Pocket Jeans

Five pocket jeans are the most common type of jeans on the market. However, the original Levi Strauss & Co. prototype, which was produced in 1873, only had three pockets (two on the front and one at the back). It was not until 1905 that Levi's added a watch pocket (coin pocket) inside the front right pocket and a final back pocket to their 501XX jeans.

BACK POCKETS

Traditional

Carpenter

No Pockets

Oval-shaped

Embellished

Western Style Pockets with Flaps

Flap Pockets with Buttons

Patch Pockets with Zippers

FRONT POCKETS

Traditional Five Pocket

Stitched Round Pocket

Patch Pocket

Embellished Pocket

Mitered Patch Pocket

TO WEAR DREAMS
ON ONE'S FEET IS
TO BEGIN TO GIVE
A REALITY TO
ONE'S DREAMS.

/ ROGER VIVIER

04 ACCESSORIES

—————

HAT AND CAP / MASK / EYEWEAR /
TIE / SCARF / BAG / WALLET / WATCH /
GLOVES / HAND FAN / BELT / HOSIERY
(SOCKS, STOCKINGS AND TIGHTS) /
SHOES / GEM / RING / BODY PIERCING
AND EARRINGS / NECKLACE /
BRACELET / OTHER ACCESSORIES

4.1 **HAT AND CAP**

Fedora

Typically made of felt with a wide brim, the fedora hat is distinguished by its lengthwise crease down the crown and pinched sides. Soaring to popularity after it was introduced in 1891, it soon eclipsed the similar-looking but dressier homburg hat.

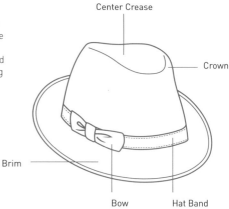

Center Crease

Crown

Brim

Bow

Hat Band

HAT & CAP TYPES

Top Hat

Bowler

Trilby
narrow brim that is snapped down at the front and turned up at the back

Homburg

Porkpie

Tyrolean

Deerstalker

Cloche

Breton

Panama
rounder and taller than a fedora

Deerstalker

Commonly made of wool tweed, the deerstalker hat is constructed from six or eight triangular panels with round edges which are sewn together. It is typically worn for hunting in rural areas, especially for deer stalking. Made famous by Sherlock Holmes, who is always seen wearing a deerstalker in the novels and movies, this type of hat hence became the standard headgear for detectives.

ACCESSORIES

Hat / Mask / Eyewear / Tie / Scarf / Bag / Wallet / Watch / Gloves / Fan / Belt / Hosiery / Shoes / Gem / Ring / Earring / Necklace / Bracelet / Others

Fedora

Cartwheel Hat
always has a lower crown
than a picture hat

Picture Hat
has a wide brim
with decorations

Floppy Hat

Jockey Cap

Pillbox

Pillbox with Veil

Bucket Hat

Tulip Hat

Mushroom Hat
with a brim facing
down

Boater

Straw Hat

Juliet Cap

Bonnet

Fascinator

Flat Cap

Tweed Flat Cap

Newsboy Cap
rounder and fuller
than a flat cap

Beret

Tam o' Shanter

Nightcap

Phrygian Cap

Crochet Hat

Rasta Hat
a colorful cap which
can be knitted, woven
or sewn

Beanie

Toque

Bobble Hat

Ushanka

Cossack Cap

Russian
Trapper

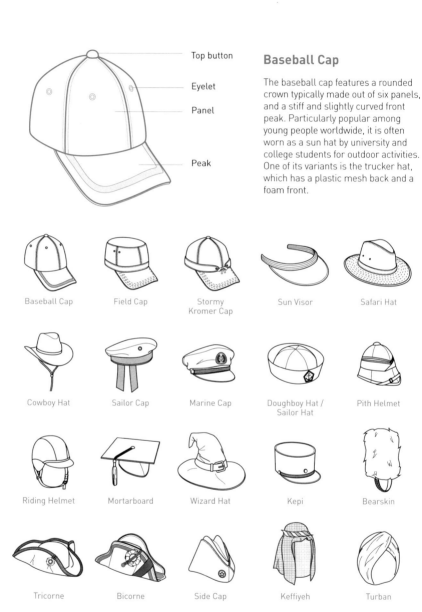

Top button

Eyelet

Panel

Peak

Baseball Cap

The baseball cap features a rounded crown typically made out of six panels, and a stiff and slightly curved front peak. Particularly popular among young people worldwide, it is often worn as a sun hat by university and college students for outdoor activities. One of its variants is the trucker hat, which has a plastic mesh back and a foam front.

Baseball Cap

Field Cap

Stormy Kromer Cap

Sun Visor

Safari Hat

Cowboy Hat

Sailor Cap

Marine Cap

Doughboy Hat / Sailor Hat

Pith Helmet

Riding Helmet

Mortarboard

Wizard Hat

Kepi

Bearskin

Tricorne

Bicorne

Side Cap

Keffiyeh

Turban

Fez

Coolie Hat

Sombrero

169

ACCESSORIES

Hat / **Mask** / Eyewear / Tie / Scarf / Bag / Wallet / Watch / Gloves / Fan / Belt / Hosiery / Shoes / Gem / Ring / Earring / Necklace / Bracelet / Others

4.2 **MASK**

Domino Mask

Traditionally worn at the Venetian Carnival, the domino mask is a type of small, half mask which covers only the eyes and the surrounding area. It is very similar to the Colombina mask, which offers slightly more coverage. The domino mask is occasionally dubbed the 'burglar mask' or 'bandit mask', as it is often worn by either thieves or superheroes in comics to conceal their identities.

MASK TYPES

Medico Della Peste

Volto (Larva)

Colombina

Zanni

Traditional Africa Mask

Japanese Hannya

Welding Mask

Ski Mask

Gas Mask

Chinese Opera Mask

In Beijing opera performances, Beijing opera masks are painted with colorful facial makeup, with each color symbolizing a different meaning and characteristic of the role. 'Face changing' is a famous trick in which the performer changes their mask in front of the audience in the blink of an eye. The art is regarded as a national secret as it requires masterful technique which remains a mystery to the public.

4.3 EYEWEAR

Aviator Sunglasses

First introduced in 1936 for U.S. military pilots, the aviator sunglasses' original form featured large, slightly convex lenses that bent around the human eye for all-rounded protection. It became widely popular along with the rise of the hippie counterculture, where large metallic sunglasses were a major trend.

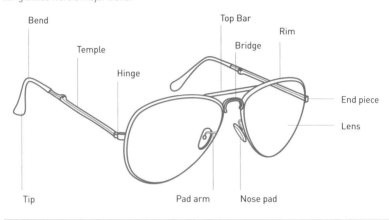

FRAME SHAPES

Round

Boston

Wellington

Lexington

Oval

Flat Top

Rimless

Top Rimless

Square

Half Eye

Foxy

Aviator

Teardrop

Octagon

Pentagon

Heart

Shield

Caged

Shutter Shade

Cat Eye

ACCESSORIES

Hat / Mask / **Eyewear** / Tie / Scarf / Bag / Wallet / Watch / Gloves / Fan / Belt / Hosiery / Shoes / Gem / Ring / Earring / Necklace / Bracelet / Others

Horn-rimmed Glasses

Originally made of authentic horn or tortoiseshell, horn-rimmed glasses are more often than not made of thick acetate or plastic that imitate those materials. One of the first types of eyeglasses to become a trendy fashion item, horn-rimmed glasses have become popular since 1917 after comedian Harold Lloyd began wearing a rounded pair in his movies.

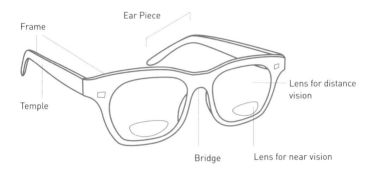

Frame

Ear Piece

Temple

Lens for distance vision

Bridge

Lens for near vision

GLASSES TYPES

Horn-rimmed Glasses / Wayfarer

Half Rim

Rimless

Bifocal

Half Rim Glasses

Foldable

Teashades / Granny Glasses

Aviator

Sunglasses

Wrap Around

Clip-on Sunglasses

Bike Glasses

Combination
with a frame made of metal and plastic for different parts

Pince-nez

Lorgnette

Shutter Shade

Safety Spectacles

Monocle

Google Glasses

Goggles

4.4 **TIE**

Tie

A component of formal attire for men, a tie is also a compulsory part of many school and work uniforms. Traditionally, and for more proper occasions, the top button of the shirt should be fastened when wearing a tie, with the tie knot resting between the two collar points. A more casual alternative is to have the tie knotted loosely around the neck with the top shirt button undone.

Shell

Rolled Edge

Hem

Tipping (at the back)

Bow Tie

Cross Knot

Wing

Continental Tie

Shirt Collar

Neckband

Snap / Pin

Bolo Tie

Slide

Cord

Aglet

TIE TYPES

Tie

Club Tie

British Regimental Tie

American Regimental Tie

Knit Tie

Bow Tie

Cravat

Ribbon Tie

Lavallière

Continental Tie

4.5 **SCARF**

Scarf

A scarf is an item of clothing worn around the neck or close to the head for various purposes, such as for warmth, cleanliness, fashion or religious reasons. Scarves worn for cleanliness or religious reasons are commonly made of more breathable, sheer and softer textiles in triangular or rectangular shapes, while those worn for warmth are usually made of wool, and sometimes real animal skins and fur.

Variants of fur scarves include boas, fur collars and zibellinos. As styling accessories, fabric scarves can be worn and tied in various ways.

SCARF TYPES

Shawl

Stole

Muffler

Headscarf

called *hijab* in
Islamic cultures

Babushka

Fur Collar

Shoulder Wrap

Capelet

Shrug

Snood Circle /
Infinity Scarf

Zibellino

Boa

long round scarf made of
feather, pleated silk or fur

Bandana

Crochet
Ascot Scarf

4.6 **BAG**

COMMON BAG SILHOUETTES

Clutch

Saddle

Baguette

Hobo

Bowling

Duffle

Tote

Backpack

Messenger

Bucket

Doctor

175

ACCESSORIES

Hat / Mask / Eyewear / Tie / Scarf / **Bag** / Wallet / Watch / Gloves / Fan / Belt / Hosiery / Shoes / Gem / Ring / Earring / Necklace / Bracelet / Others

Handbag

Purses were initially used by early modern Europeans, both men and women, for carrying coins. Made of leather or soft fabric, they were always very small in size. During the Industrial Revolution in England, increased railway travel led to the demand for larger-sized bags as purses were too small and the materials were not durable enough for the journey.

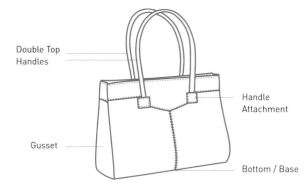

Double Top Handles

Gusset

Handle Attachment

Bottom / Base

BAG TYPES

Bracelet Bag

Clutch

Minaudière

Evening Bag

Envelope Clutch

Kiss Lock Handbag

Pochette

Box Bag

Pompadour Bag

Sporran

Bermuda Bag

Sally Jess Bag

Inro

Muff Bag

Tote Bag

Hobo Bag

Canteen Bag

Pannier Bag

Satchel

Chanel Bag

Medicine Bag

Accordion / Compartment Bag

Bucket Bag

Squaw Bag

Saddle Bag

Straw Bag / Beach Bag

Backpack

Hang Loop

Zippe

Shoulder Strap

Outsic Pocke

Bottom / Base

Woven Tote Bag

Kenya Bag

Basket

Hat Box

Lunchbox Bag

Shopping Bag

Belt Bag

Waist Bag / Belt Pack

Sling Bag

Doctor Bag

Duffle Bag

Boston Bag

Gladstone Bag

Weekender

Boxer Bag

Roll Bag

Bowling Bag

Courier Bag / Messenger Bag

Tennis Bag

Golf Bag

Messenger Bag

The modern-day messenger bag originated from the utility lineman's bag manufactured by De Martini Globe Canvas Company in the 1950s, which was designed for linemen to keep essential gear and tools easily accessible while climbing utility poles.

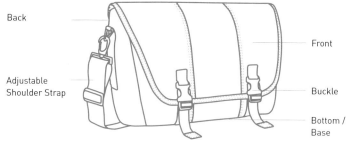

Back

Front

Adjustable
Shoulder Strap

Buckle

Bottom /
Base

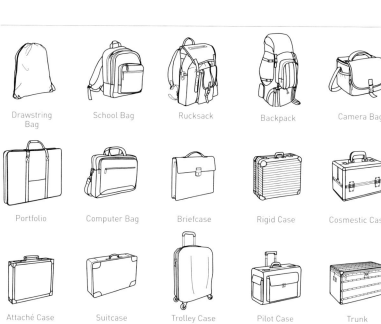

Drawstring
Bag

School Bag

Rucksack

Backpack

Camera Bag

Portfolio

Computer Bag

Briefcase

Rigid Case

Cosmestic Case

Attaché Case

Suitcase

Trolley Case

Pilot Case

Trunk

Kelly Bag

Hailed as a symbol of status, the Hermès Kelly bag got its name when Grace Kelly, the Princess of Monaco, was spotted using the handbag to shield her baby bump from the paparazzi. After the photo was published, the bag quickly received attention and gained popularity.

4.7 **WALLET**

Wallet

A wallet is a small, typically pocket-sized and portable flat case used for carrying cash, identity cards, bank cards, photographs, etc.

WALLET TYPES

Continental Wallet

Bifold Wallet

Trifold Wallet

Credit Card Wallet

Purse

Coin Purse

Key Case

Spectacle Case

Business Card Holder

Card Holder

Writing Case

Money Clip

4.8 **WATCH**

Chronograph Watch

First introduced in 1816, the chronograph watch is a type of mechanical watch that combines the functions of a stopwatch and a display watch, originally designed for tracking astronomical objects. Besides its core time-telling and stopwatch functions, many specialized chronographs feature intricate detailing and complex features, and as a result cost considerably more than the basic types. Nowadays, chronograph watches are widely used in car racing, diving, and for navigating aircraft and submarines.

Strap
Link
Minute Hand
Axis
Hour Hand
Bezel
Dial Ring
Luminous Marker
Crown
Dial
Pusher
Second Hand
Sub-dial

SHAPES

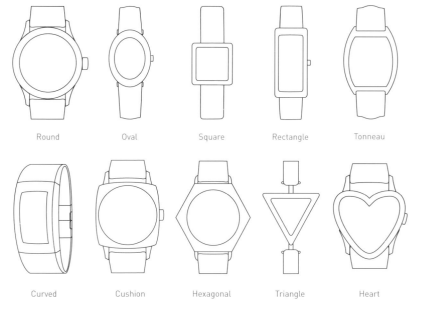

Round

Oval

Square

Rectangle

Tonneau

Curved

Cushion

Hexagonal

Triangle

Heart

Strap
Link
Crystal
Minute Hand
Bezel

Crown Guard
Hour Hand
Crown
Second Hand
Lug
Date Window

FASHIONARY
50 metres

Dive Watch

Dive watches are water-resistant watches designed
for use during diving. Modern dive watches must
conform to ISO 6425 standards, which regulate
and attribute watch models that are suitable for
underwater diving to a minimum depth of 100m.

Digital / Sport Watch

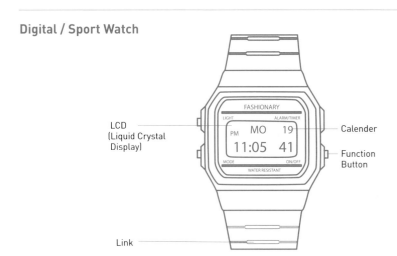

LCD
(Liquid Crystal
Display)

Link

Calender

Function
Button

FASHIONARY
LIGHT   ALARM/TIMER
PM   MO   19
11:05 41
MODE   ON/OFF
WATER RESISTANT

Pocket Watch

Case Bow

Stem

Case Frame

Front Cover

Crystal

STRAPS

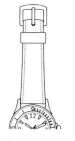

Leather Strap

Stainless Steel
Link Bracelet

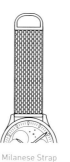

Milanese Strap

Chain Watch
Strap

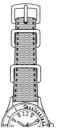

Woven Strap

Nato Strap

Expandable
Strap

Sport Band

4.9 **GLOVES**

Driving Gloves

Driving gloves were initially used to keep motor car drivers' hands clean, because racing cars in the early days usually used wooden steering wheels taken directly from road cars. Modern driving gloves are made of soft, thin leather to minimise stress. They are designed with short cuffs to enable more movement, and feature openings at the knuckles and back of the hands for maximized flexibility. As fashionable as they are functional, both full-finger and fingerless driving gloves have become popular accessories among street dancers.

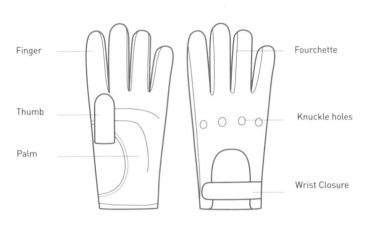

Finger

Thumb

Palm

Fourchette

Knuckle holes

Wrist Closure

GLOVE TYPES

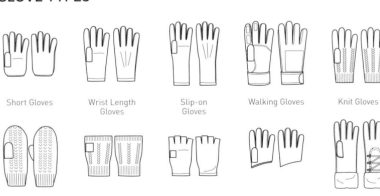

Short Gloves

Wrist Length Gloves

Slip-on Gloves

Walking Gloves

Knit Gloves

Mittens

Fingerless Mittens

Fingerless Gloves

Half Gloves

Igloo Gloves

183

ACCESSORIES

Hat / Mask / Eyewear / Tie / Scarf / Bag / Wallet / Watch / **Gloves** / Fan / Belt / Hosiery / Shoes / Gem / Ring / Earring / Necklace / Bracelet / Others

Opera Gloves

Opera gloves are a type of formal, elbow-length gloves that are tight-fitting to such an extent that women often need the help of talcum powder and buttonhooks to put them on. They are alternatively known as the Mousquetaire because of the openings at the wrists, which are fastened by a three-button or snap closure. In the 17th to 19th centuries, it was regarded as bad etiquette to put on or take off gloves entirely in public, so women would unbutton the Mousquetaire openings to slip their palms out, while tidily folding in the gloves' finger sections.

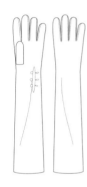

Long Gloves

Long Arm Gloves

Fingerless Long Gloves

Gauntlets

Muff / Handwarmer

Archer's Gloves

Oven Gloves

4.10 **HAND FAN**

Pleated Fan

A type of folding fan made of a pleated curved leaf of paper, lace, silk or other sheer materials, which is glued onto two sticks of identical lengths riveted together at the end.

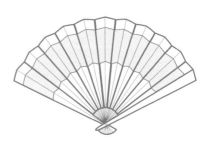

Jenny Lind Fan

Similar in structure as the brise fan, the Jenny Lind fan is also known as the petal fan, due to the petal-shaped leaf attached to every rib. When opened up, the fan appears to have a single connected fan leaf. The petal leaves can be made of a variety of materials, such as silk, lace, paper and feathers.

HAND FAN TYPES

Brise Fan

Cockade Fan

Trifold Fan

Uchiwa Fan

Chinese Fixed Fan

Fixed Feather Fan

Comfyhold Fan

Thumbhold Fan

4.11 **BELT**

Belt

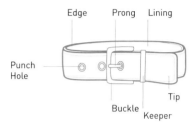

Edge Prong Lining

Punch Hole

Buckle Keeper

Tip

Suspenders

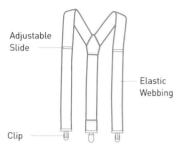

Adjustable Slide

Elastic Webbing

Clip

BELT TYPES

D-Ring Belt

Mesh Metal Belt

Grommet Belt

Surcingle Belt

a woven belt with a leather tab and metal buckle

Braided Leather Belt

Webbing Belt with Cam Buckle

Metal Stretch Belt

Ribbon Belt

Snake Belt

Western Belt

Cinch Belt

Concha Belt

Safari Belt

Cartridge Belt

Money Belt

Cummerbund

Polo Belt

Kidney Belt

Obi Belt

Sash Belt

Ring Belt

Chain Belt

String Belt

Sam Browne Belt

Suspenders

4.12 **HOSIERY**
SOCKS, STOCKINGS AND TIGHTS

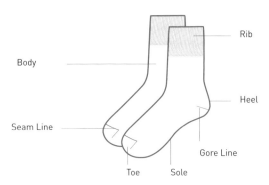

Rib

Body

Heel

Seam Line

Gore Line

Toe   Sole

SOCK TYPES

Foot Socks /
No-show socks

Sneaker Socks

Ankle Socks

Crew Socks

Bobby Socks
socks with thick uppers that
are turned down to form a
thick cuff at ankle height

Knee-high
Socks

Over-the-knee Socks

Loose Socks

Thong Socks /
Tabi

Toe Socks

Leg Warmer

Traditionally designed for keeping ballerinas' legs warm, leg warmers have
nowadays become a fashion item with both functional and styling purposes.
They can be mixed and matched with a variety of footwear and leggings,
such as layered inside or outside boots, over leggings and stockings, etc.
New parents have also found leg warmers useful for keeping babies and
toddlers warm while changing their diapers.

STOCKING & TIGHT TYPES

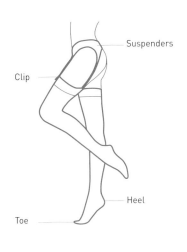

Suspenders

Clip

Heel

Toe

Tights /
Pantyhose

Control Tights

Tattoo Tights

Hold-ups

Seamed Stockings

Nylon-made seamed stockings were greatly popular in the 1940s, but production was halted a mere one month after its launch due to World War II. American women came up with the idea of paint-on hosiery to imitate the appearance of seamed stockings - covering the length with nude-tone cosmetics and then drawing on a 'seam' at the back with an eyebrow pencil.

Open Toe Tights

Bare Invisible
Tights

Stockings &
Suspenders

Fishnet Tights

Footless Tights

Knee-high
Stockings

Calf-high
Stockings

4.13 **SHOES**

Oxford

Historically from Scotland, and once named in Balmorals after the Balmoral Castle, Oxford shoes were later on famously renamed after Oxford University. Oxfords are defined by their construction of a "close-lacing".

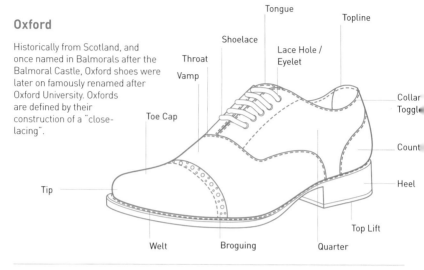

Tongue
Topline
Shoelace
Throat
Lace Hole / Eyelet
Vamp
Collar
Toggle
Toe Cap
Count
Heel
Tip
Top Lift
Welt
Broguing
Quarter

FLATS

Ballet Flat

Folding Ballet Flat / Pixie Flat

Espadrille

Slip-on

Thong

Clog

Mule

d'Orsay Flat

Opera Pump

Boat Shoe / Deck Shoe

Moccasin

Mary Jane

Initially known as bar shoes, the term Mary Jane was introduced in 1904, when the Brown Shoe Company started marketing this type of shoes after the popular comic characters Buster Brown and his sister Mary Jane.

Wallabee

Loafer

Penny Loafer

Brogue

Buck

Spectator

Balmoral / Galosh Oxford

Monkstrap

Derby

Blucher

Wingtip

ACCESSORIES

Hat / Mask / Eyewear / Tie / Scarf / Bag / Wallet / Watch / Gloves / Fan / Belt / Hosiery / **Shoes** / Gem / Ring / Earring / Necklace / Bracelet / Others

SANDALS

Flip-flop

Slide Sandal

Ankle Strap Sandal

Slingback Thong

Huarache

Gladiator

Fisherman Sandal

Flatform

Cork Sandal

Espadrille Wedge

HIGH HEEL SHOES

Pump

Pointy Pump

Mary Jane Pump

Stiletto

d'Orsay Pump

Slingback

T-Bar

Peep Toe Pump

Mule

Platform

Wedge

Oxford Pump

Kiltie Pump

Heel-less

Lita Boot

Stiletto

Named after the stiletto dagger, owing to the resemblance in its silhouette, the stiletto heel refers to a type of thin, narrow high heel usually found on women's boots and shoes. Favoured for the optical illusion it gives - longer and more slender legs, tinier feet, greater height and more flattering proportions - the stiletto is often featured in popular culture partly due to its seductive image.

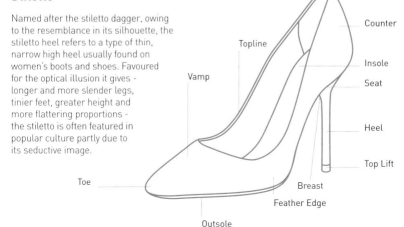

Topline

Vamp

Counter

Insole

Seat

Heel

Top Lift

Toe

Breast

Feather Edge

Outsole

Athletic Shoe

Athletic shoes typically feature a flexible sole and deeper tread to provide traction, with additional elements under the heel to enhance shock absorption. Nowadays due to the expansion of the industry and designs, the name "athletic shoes" is mostly based on the design of the shoe sole rather than the upper.

BOOTS

Flat Shoe Boot

Ankle Boot

Chukka

Desert Boot

Multi-buckle Boot

Steel-toe Boot

Dress Boot

Duck Boot

Work Boot

Australian Boot

Hiking Boot

Jodhpur Boot

Deck Boot

Harness Boot

Pecos Boot

Chelsea / Side Gore Boot

Chelsea boots, characterized by elastic side gores, can be traced back to the Victorian era when they were worn by men and women alike. Shoemaker Anello & Davide reimagined the Chelsea boots in the 1960s with cuban heels and pointed toes for The Beatles. This variant became known as the Beatle boots.

191

ACCESSORIES

Hat / Mask / Eyewear / Tie / Scarf / Bag / Wallet / Watch / Gloves / Fan / Belt / Hosiery / **Shoes** / Gem / Ring / Earring / Necklace / Bracelet / Others

Logger Boot

UGG Boot

Indian Boot /
Moccasin Boot

Rigger Boot

Mukluk

Tanker Boot

Snow Boot /
Moon Boot

Cowboy Boot

Galoshe /
Wellington Boot

Slouch Boot

ATHLETIC SHOES & SNEAKERS

Plimsoll

Vans Slip-on

Low-top
Converse

High-top
Converse

Hiking Shoe

Tennis Shoe

Soccer Shoe

Running Shoe

Bowling Shoe

Basketball Shoe

TOE TYPES

Pointed Toe

Almond Toe

Square Toe

Shell Toe

Peep Toe

Wing Tip

Bicycle Toe

Cap Toe

Perf Toe

HEEL TYPES

Flat Heel

Dutch Heel

Concealed /
Secret Heel

French Heel

Wedge Heel

Stiletto Heel

4.14 **GEM**

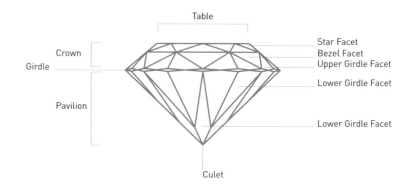

HARDNESS OF DIFFERENT GEMS

MINERAL	HARDNESS SCALE	SCRATCH TEST	OTHER FACTS
Talc	1	scratchable with fingernail	used in talcum powder
Gypsum	2	scratchable with fingernail	ingredient of plaster
Calcite	3	scratchable with copper coin	used in cement
Fluorite	4	scratchable with nail	used in toothpaste
Apatite	5	scratchable with nail	mineral in bones
Feldspar	6	scratch with porcelain tile	ingredient of glass
Quartz	7	scratches window glass	ingredient of glass
Topaz	8	scratches glass	gems
Corundum	9	scratches topas	rubies & sapphires
Diamond	10	scratches corundum	used in rings

GEM CUTS

Round Brilliant Cut   Oval Cut   Pear Cut   Marquise Cut   Heart Cut   Cushion Cut

ACCESSORIES

Hat / Mask / Eyewear / Tie / Scarf / Bag / Wallet / Watch / Gloves / Fan / Belt / Hosiery / Shoes / **Gem** / Ring / Earring / Necklace / Bracelet / Others

Rectangle
Step Cut

Square
Step Cut

Round Hexagonal
Step Cut

Emerald
Cut

Baguette Cut

Tapered
Baguette Cut

Scissor Cut

Round
Hexagonal
Scissor Cut

Oval
Hexagonal
Scissor Cut

Radiant Cut

Princess Cut

Trillion Cut

Old Mine Cut

Eight Cut

Asscher Cut

French Cut

Table Cut

Point Cut

Half Dutch
Rose Cut

Dutch
Rose Cut

Double
Rose Cut

Three-facet
Rose Cut

Six-facet
Rose Cut

Antwerp
Rose Cut

Briolette Cut

Faceted
Teardrop Cut

Flat
Cabochon
Cut

Cabochon Cut

Smooth Cut
Plain Sphere

Smooth Cut
Teardrop

4.15 **RING**

Engagement Ring Set

A matching set consisting of an engagement ring and a wedding band that complement each other. The engagement ring is worn after an engagement and before the wedding, and the wedding band is worn after the wedding ceremony. Some brides choose to wear only the wedding band after the ceremony, while others may opt to weld the two together.
A larger, set center stone is commonly found on engagement rings, whereas wedding bands usually use smaller pavé stones.

Engagement Ring

Wedding Band

GEM SETTINGS

Bar Setting

Channel Setting

Pavé / Bead Setting

Bezel Setting

Prong Setting

Invisible Setting

Flush Setting

Tension Setting

RING TYPES

Solitaire Ring

Tension Ring

Flush Setting
Ring

Bezel Ring

Halo Ring

Band Ring

Charm Ring

Posy Ring

Spiral Ring

Triple Ring

Crossover Ring

Puzzle Ring

Irish Claddagh Ring

Fede Ring

Round Ring

Peace Ring

Poison Ring
with a container under
or inside the bezel

College Ring

Hollow Ring

Spoon Ring

Signet Ring

Sovereign Ring
has a gold sovereign
as primary decorative feature

Eternity Ring

An eternity ring is a type of women's ring, normally gifted to the wife by her husband on a special occasion or significant anniversary, such as a 50th anniversary. It is a precious metal band of gold or silver, set with a continuous pavé line of identical gems, typically diamonds, to symbolize eternal love.
The concept was conceived in the 1960s as a means of promoting smaller diamonds of less than 0.25 carats. Marketing strategies involved campaign slogans targeting husbands, with the most famous one being "She married you for richer or poorer. Let her know how it's going", which made the idea greatly popular.

RING SIZE CHART

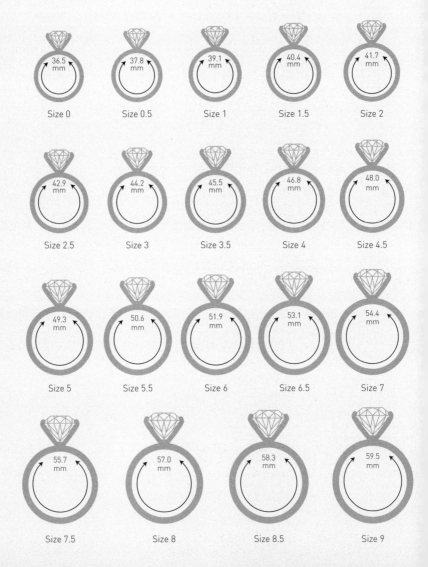

36.5 mm	37.8 mm	39.1 mm	40.4 mm	41.7 mm
Size 0	Size 0.5	Size 1	Size 1.5	Size 2
42.9 mm	44.2 mm	45.5 mm	46.8 mm	48.0 mm
Size 2.5	Size 3	Size 3.5	Size 4	Size 4.5
49.3 mm	50.6 mm	51.9 mm	53.1 mm	54.4 mm
Size 5	Size 5.5	Size 6	Size 6.5	Size 7
55.7 mm	57.0 mm	58.3 mm	59.5 mm	
Size 7.5	Size 8	Size 8.5	Size 9	

Size 9.5

Size 10

Size 10.5

Size 11

Size 11.5

Size 12

Size 12.5

Size 13

Size 13.5

Size 14

Size 14.5

Size 15

Size 15.5

Size 16

4.16 BODY PIERCING AND EARRINGS

COMMON BODY PIERCING POSITIONS

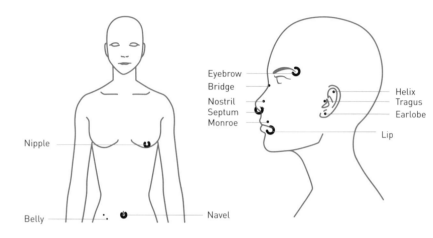

DIFFERENT BODY PIERCING RINGS AND BARS

LIP PIERCINGS

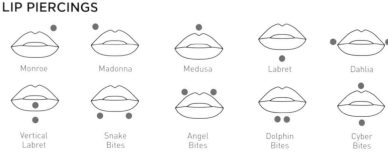

EARRING TYPES

Hoop Earring

Drop Earring

hung just below the earlobe
and is often stationary or
moves very little

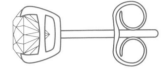

Stud Earring

A stud earring is the most basic type of earring for
pierced ears. A gem or ornament is mounted on
a narrow post, which is inserted through an ear
piercing and held in place by a clutch back on the
other side, creating the impression of the ornament
floating in front of the ear. Besides being a favoured
accessory for its simple design, it is also commonly
used in other parts of the body.

Dangle Earring

Tassel Earring

Chain Ear Cuff

Chain Ear Wire

EARRING FASTENERS

Snap Back

Hinged Earwire

Screw Back

Clip-on

Omega Back /
French Clip Back

Fish Hook

4.17 **NECKLACE**

LENGTHS OF NECKLACE

Choker 14"
Collar 16"
Princess 18"
Matinee 24"
Opera 30"
Rope 33"

CLASP TYPES

Lobster Clasp

Swivel Lobster
Clasp

Spring Ring

Toggle Clasp

Bayonet Clasp

Figure 8
Safety Clasp

Open Box Clasp

Snap Clasp

Magnetic Clasp

S-Hook

Slide Clasp

Pearl Clasp

Barrel Clasp

201

ACCESSORIES

Hat / Mask / Eyewear / Tie / Scarf / Bag / Wallet / Watch / Gloves / Fan / Belt / Hosiery / Shoes / Gem / Ring / Earring / **Necklace** / Bracelet / Others

NECKLACE TYPES

Pendant

Cross Pendant

Crusader's Cross

Medallion
Necklace

Solitaire Necklace

Locket Pendant

Tassel Pendant

Y-Necklace

Lariat Necklace

Invisible Necklace

Statement Necklace

Graduated Necklace

Neck Ring /
Torc Necklace

Collar

Egyptian Collar

Esclavage Necklace

Sautoir

Beggar Beads

4.18 **BRACELET**

Charm Bracelet

A type of jewellery worn around the wrist, a charm bracelet is decorated with 'charms' of personal significance, such as ornaments, pendants or trinkets that symbolize important events or things in the wearer's life. Renowned jeweller Tiffany & Co. launched their first charm bracelet in 1889 - a link bracelet with a single dangling heart charm - which has now become an iconic design of the brand.

BRACELET TYPES

Cuff

Bangle

Hinged
Bangle

Tennis
Bracelet

Friendship
Bracelet

Chain
Bracelet

Charm
Bracelet

Coiled
Bracelet

Snake
Bracelet

Sport
Wristband

Leather
Wristband

Spring
Bracelet

Slide
Bracelet

Bead Bracelet

Scarab
Bracelet

Expandable
Bracelet

Elastic
Bracelet

Identity
Bracelet

Smart
Bracelet

Bracelet
Ring

4.19 **OTHER ACCESSORIES**

Body Wire / Body Tattoo

Stick-on Body Jewelry

Anklet

Toe-ankle Chain

Armlet

Collar Chain

Collar Tips

Collar Pins

Tie Pin

Lapel Pin

Brooch

Regimental Badge

Cufflinks

Hat Pin

I LIKE LIGHT,
COLOR,
LUMINOSITY.
I LIKE THINGS FULL
OF COLOR
AND VIBRANT.

/ OSCAR DE LA RENTA

05 TEXTILE

FIBER / YARN / FABRIC (WOVEN, KNIT & NONWOVEN) / LEATHER / LACE / FINISHING (DYEING & PRINTING) / FABRIC PATTERN / ORGANIC TEXTILE / FABRIC SELECTION GUIDE / FABRIC DICTIONARY

5.1 **FIBER**

NATURAL FIBER CLASSIFICATION

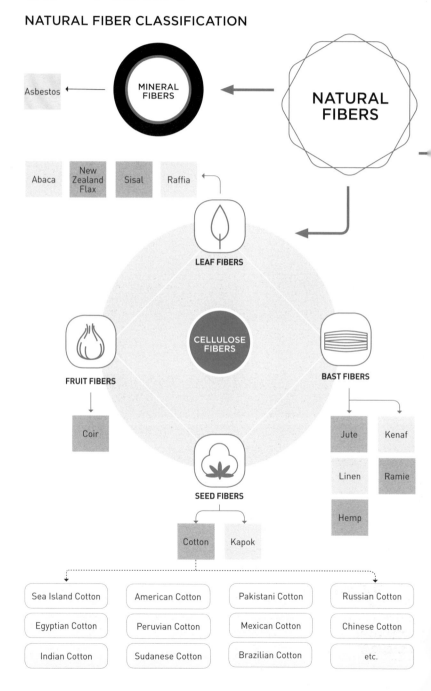

TEXTILE

Fiber / Yarn / Fabric / Leather / Lace / Finishing / Fabric Pattern / Organic Textile / Fabric Selection Guide / Fabric Dictionary

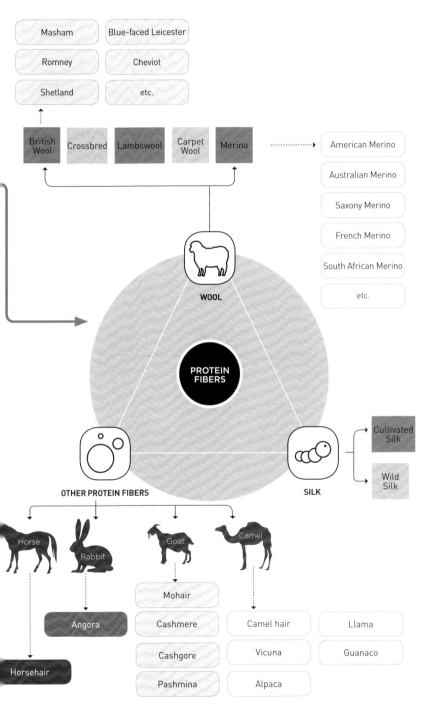

MANMADE FIBER CLASSIFICATION

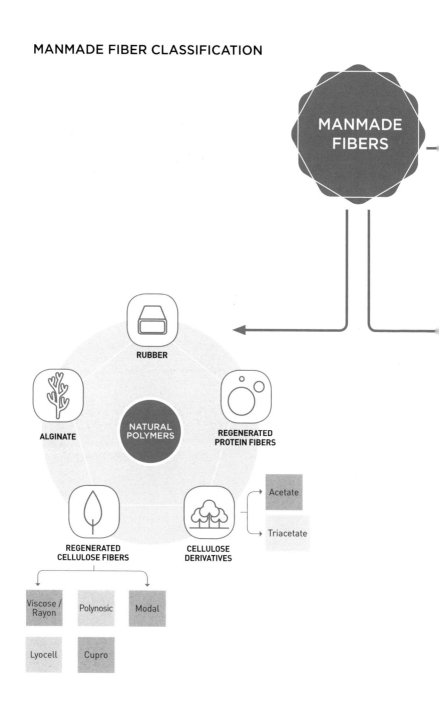

MANMADE
FIBERS

NATURAL
POLYMERS

RUBBER

ALGINATE

REGENERATED
PROTEIN FIBERS

REGENERATED
CELLULOSE FIBERS

CELLULOSE
DERIVATIVES

Acetate

Triacetate

Viscose /
Rayon

Polynosic

Modal

Lyocell

Cupro

TEXTILE

Fiber / Yarn / Fabric / Leather / Lace / Finishing / Fabric Pattern / Organic Textile / Fabric Selection Guide / Fabric Dictionary

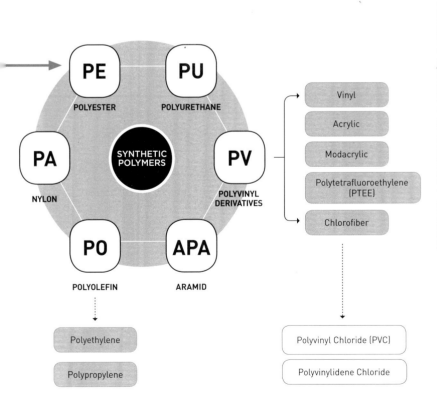

COMMON FIBER PROPERTIES

	NATURAL FIBERS			
	Cotton	Linen	Wool	Silk
Moisture Absorption	💧💧	💧💧💧	💧💧💧	💧💧💧
Mold Resistance	✹	✹✹	✹✹✹	✹✹✹
Max. Temperature of Ironing (°C)	200°C	230°C	150°C	150°C
UV Resistance	☀☀	☀☀☀	☀☀☀	☀
Handfeel	😊	😐	😊	😊
Anti-abrasion	⩘⩘⩘	⩘⩘	⩘⩘	⩘
Anti-pilling	☆☆☆	☆☆☆	☆☆	☆☆☆
Resilience	★	★	★★★	★★
Electrical Conductivity	⚡	⚡	⚡⚡	⚡⚡
Thermoplastic	✕	✕	✕	✕

MAN-MADE FIBERS

Acetate	Viscose / Rayon	Acrylic	Nylon	Polyolefin	Polyester
160°C	180°C	150°C	180°C	120°C	160°C

FIBER NAMES IN DIFFERENT LANGUAGES

CODE	ENGLISH	FRENCH	GERMAN	ITALIAN
AC	Acetate	Acétate	Acetat	Acetato
PC	Acrylic	Acrylique	Acryl	Acrilico
WA	Angora	Angora	Angora	Angora
WS	Cashmere	Cachemire	Kaschmir	Cachemire
CO	Cotton	Coton	Baumwolle	Cotone
LI	Linen	Lin	Leinen	Lino
PA	Nylon	Nylon	Nylon	Nylon
PE	Polyester	Polyester	Polyester	Poliestere
PU	Polyurethane (Spandex / Lycra)	Polyuréthane	Polyurethan	Poliuretano
RA	Ramie	Ramie	Ramie	Ramiè
VI	Rayon	Rayonne	Kunstseide	Raion
SE	Silk	Soie	Seide	Seta
WO	Wool	Laine	Wolle	Lana

TEXTILE

Fiber / Yarn / Fabric / Leather / Lace / Finishing / Fabric Pattern / Organic Textile / Fabric Selection Guide / Fabric Dictionary

SPANISH	CHINESE	JAPANESE	KOREAN
Acetato	醋酯 / 醋纖	アセテート	아세테이트
Acrílico	聚丙烯腈 / 腈綸 / 人造毛	アクリル	아크릴
Angora	安哥拉兔毛 / 兔毛	アンゴラ	앙고라
Cachemira	開司米 / 羊絨	カシミヤ	캐시미어 천
Algodón	棉	棉 (コットン)	면
Lino	亞麻	亞麻 (リネン)	리넨
Nylon	尼龍	ナイロン	나일론
Poliéster	聚酯 / 滌綸	ポリエステル	폴리 에스테르
Poliuretano	聚氨酯 / 拉架 / 氨綸	ポリウレタン	폴리 우레탄
Ramio	苎麻	苎麻 (カラムシ)	라미
Rayón	人造絲 / 黏織	レーヨン	레이온
Seda	蠶絲	絹 (シルク)	실크
Lana	羊毛	ウール	양모

5.2 **YARN**

YARN CLASSIFICATION

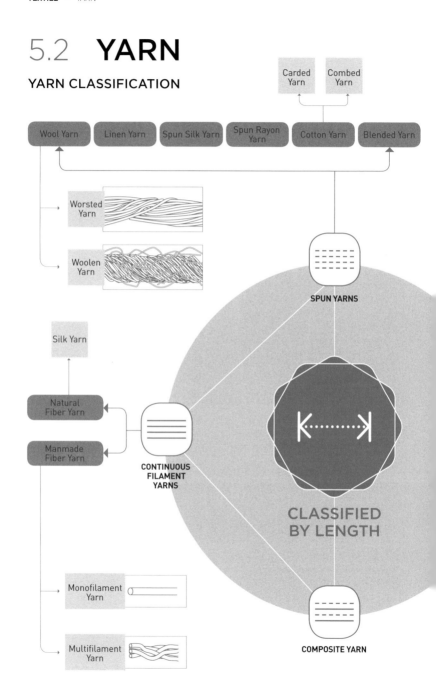

Carded Yarn

Combed Yarn

Wool Yarn | Linen Yarn | Spun Silk Yarn | Spun Rayon Yarn | Cotton Yarn | Blended Yarn

Worsted Yarn

Woolen Yarn

SPUN YARNS

Silk Yarn

Natural Fiber Yarn

Manmade Fiber Yarn

CONTINUOUS FILAMENT YARNS

Monofilament Yarn

Multifilament Yarn

CLASSIFIED BY LENGTH

COMPOSITE YARN

TEXTILE

Fiber / **Yarn** / Fabric / Leather / Lace / Finishing / Fabric Pattern / Organic Textile / Fabric Selection Guide / Fabric Dictionary

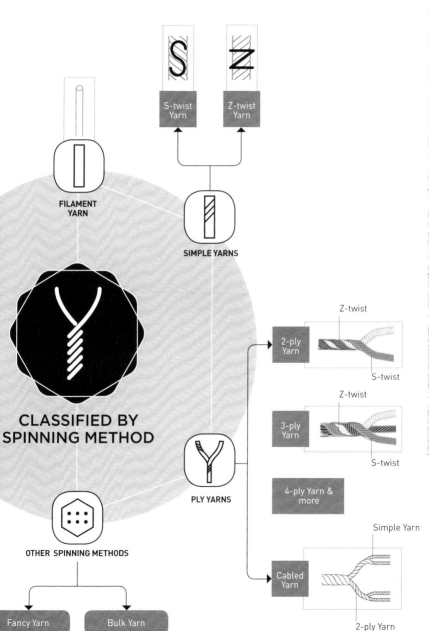

S-twist Yarn

Z-twist Yarn

FILAMENT YARN

SIMPLE YARNS

CLASSIFIED BY SPINNING METHOD

PLY YARNS

OTHER SPINNING METHODS

Fancy Yarn

Bulk Yarn

2-ply Yarn

Z-twist

S-twist

3-ply Yarn

Z-twist

S-twist

4-ply Yarn & more

Cabled Yarn

Simple Yarn

2-ply Yarn

PERFORMANCE OF DIFFERENT TYPES OF YARNS IN FABRICS

YARN TYPE	AESTHETICS	COST
SPUN YARN		
Combed Yarn	Lustrous	$$$
VS		
Carded Yarn	Loose hairy	$
Worsted Yarn	Smooth, fine	$$$
VS		
Woolen Yarn	Fuzzy, soft	$
Simple Yarn	Fuzzy, soft	$
VS		
Ply Yarn	Bulkier	$$$
CONTINUOUS FILAMENT YARN	Lustrous / Less likely to lint and pill	$$
BULK YARN	Less lustrous / Does not lint but pills easily	$$
FANCY YARN	Interesting texture / Lints & pills easily	$$$
COMPOSITE YARN	Varies depending on fiber used	Varies depending on fiber used

217

TEXTILE

Fiber / **Yarn** / Fabric / Leather / Lace / Finishing / Fabric Pattern / Organic Textile / Fabric Selection Guide / Fabric Dictionary

DURABILITY	COMFORT	CARE
Stronger — Weaker	Gentle to skin — Less gentle	Less shrinkage — More shrinkage
Stronger — Weaker	Warmer, dry to skin — Bulkier	Does not snag easily — Snags easily
Weaker — Stronger		Does not snag easily — Snags easily

👍	Stronger	😋	Cooler to skin		Snags easily
😐	Ravels easily	💧	Poor water absorbency		Does not soil easily
👍	Stronger	❄	Warmer		Snags easily
😊	Less raveling than filament yarn	💧	High water absorbency		Soils easily
👎	Weaker	❄	Warmer		Snags easily
👎	Lower abrasion resistance	💧	High water absorbency		Soils easily
	Related to Process		Varies depending on fiber used		Varies depending on fiber used

FANCY YARN

STRUCTURE OF FANCY YARN

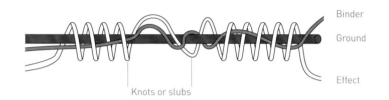

Binder

Ground

Effect

Knots or slubs

COMMON TYPES OF FANCY YARN

Marled Yarn

Spiral / Corkscrew Yarn

Bouclé Yarn

Loop Yarn

Gimp Yarn

Diamond Yarn

Snarl Yarn

Snap Yarn

Slub Yarn

Chenille Yarn

TEXTILE

Fiber / **Yarn** / Fabric / Leather / Lace / Finishing / Fabric Pattern / Organic Textile / Fabric Selection Guide / Fabric Dictionary

YARN COUNT

YARN COUNT SYSTEM

INDIRECT SYSTEM	DIRECT SYSTEM
SPUN YARNS	**CONTINUOUS FILAMENT YARNS**
/ used on all spun yarns	/ used on all continuous filament yarns
/ number of length units per unit mass	/ number of mass units per unit length.
/ higher the count number, finer the yarn lower the count number, coarser the yarn	/ higher the count number, coarser the yarn lower the count number, finer the yarn

System	Symbol	Length unit	Mass unit	Conversion formula to Nm
Cotton count	NeC/ ECC	840 yd	1 lb	C × 1.693362 C ÷ 0.590541
Metric	Nm	1 km	1 kg	/

System	Symbol	Mass unit	Length unit	Conversion formula to Nm
Denier	Td	1 g	9 km	9,000 ÷ Td
Tex	Tt	1 g	1 km	1,000 ÷ Tt

Calculation of yarn count :

$$N = \frac{L}{W} \times H$$

N = Yarn count W = Weight of standard regain
L = Length H = Length of standard hank
(constant)

Calculation of yarn count:

$$N = W \times \frac{H}{L}$$

N = Yarn number W = Weight of standard regain
L = Length H = Length of standard hank
(constant)

5.3 **FABRIC**
WOVEN, KNIT & NONWOVEN

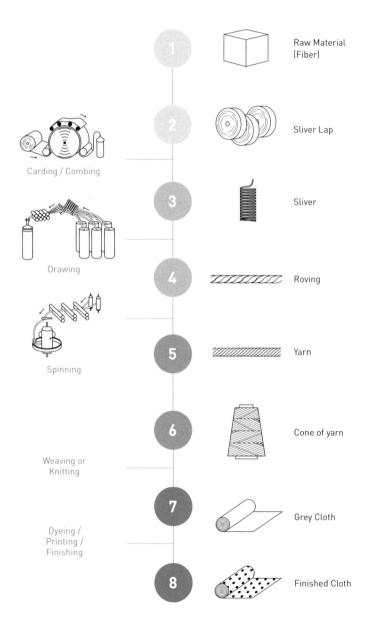

1 — Raw Material (Fiber)

2 — Sliver Lap

Carding / Combing

3 — Sliver

Drawing

4 — Roving

Spinning

5 — Yarn

6 — Cone of yarn

Weaving or Knitting

7 — Grey Cloth

Dyeing / Printing / Finishing

8 — Finished Cloth

221

TEXTILE

Fiber / Yarn / **Fabric** / Leather / Lace / Finishing / Fabric Pattern / Organic Textile / Fabric Selection Guide / Fabric Dictionary

FABRIC CLASSIFICATION

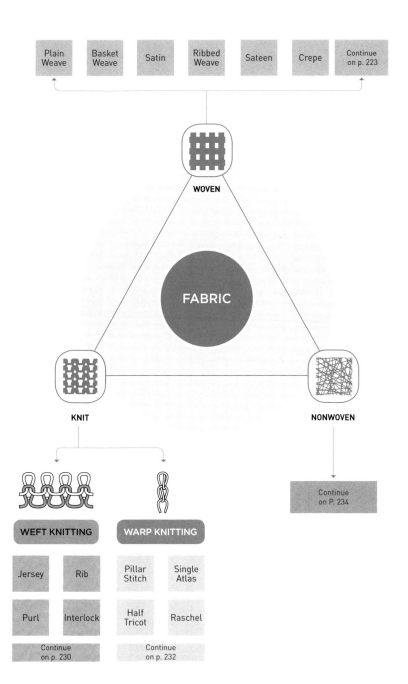

| Plain Weave | Basket Weave | Satin | Ribbed Weave | Sateen | Crepe | Continue on p. 223 |

WOVEN

FABRIC

KNIT

NONWOVEN

WEFT KNITTING

WARP KNITTING

Jersey	Rib
Purl	Interlock
Continue on p. 230	

Pillar Stitch	Single Atlas
Half Tricot	Raschel
Continue on p. 232	

Continue on P. 234

WEAVES

Weaving is one of the most common methods of textile production, forming fabric by interlacing two distinct sets of yarns or threads at right angles. The two sets of threads include the longitudinal-running 'warp' and the lateral-running 'weft' (also known as 'filling'). Different ways of interweaving these threads will result in varying characteristics of the cloth.

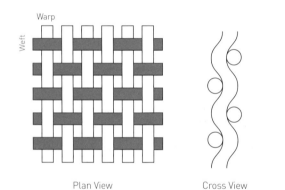

Warp

Weft

Plan View

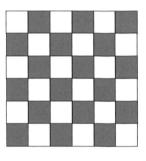

Cross View

Weave Design Structure

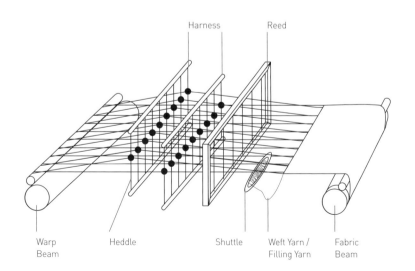

Harness

Reed

Warp
Beam

Heddle

Shuttle

Weft Yarn /
Filling Yarn

Fabric
Beam

BASIC WEAVES

NAME	PLAIN WEAVE	BASKET WEAVE	RIBBED WEAVE
PLAN VIEW			
STRUCTURE			
	Individual weft threads pass over and under each warp alternately in a square pattern.	Simultaneously interlacing two or more warps with one or more fillings, creating a more balanced structure.	Plain weave with distinct wales or cords (a ribbed pattern) woven in the warp or filling.
APPEARANCE	Usually flat with no distinct design, unless yarns of varying colors and thicknesses are used.	A variation of plain weave, basket weave creates an attractive checkerboard pattern, often using contrasting colors in the warp and weft for stronger effect.	A variation of the plain weave, it is woven with a ribbed or corded pattern for texture and design.
PROPERTIES	Easy and inexpensive to produce, offering maximum yardage. Yarn count and balance determine the durability of the fabric. Can be adapted for finishing processes, such as printing.	Inexpensive production. Drapable, absorbent, reasonably resilient and flexible. More easily soiled and less durable than plain weave.	Offers good drape. Prominent ribs affect the durability of the fabric. Tension may cause yarn slippage.
TYPICAL FABRICS	batiste, cheesecloth, cretonne, gingham, percale, voile, plaid	monk's cloth, oxford	bengaline, broadcloth, dimity, faille, poplin, rep, taffeta, grosgrain

	TWILL	SATIN	SATEEN	CREPE
PLAN VIEW				
STRUCTURE				
	Three-shaft or higher. Warp or weft floats over two or more counterpart yarns, progressively stepped up in right or left direction.	Four-shaft or higher. Warp floats in interrupted diagonal.	Four-shaft or higher. Weft floats in interrupted diagonal.	A combination of plain weave and satin or sateen.
APPEARANCE	Left- or right-hand diagonal. Variations of design include houndstooth, chevron (also known as herringbone), corkscrew, etc., which may be enhanced by colored yarns.	Smooth and compact. Interrupted diagonal visible when viewed with magnifying glass.	A variation of satin weave. Smooth and compact.	Textured, crimped and crisp surface with an irregular, indistinct pattern.
PROPERTIES	Strong and firm texture. Better drapability and resilience than plain weave, and with more interesting designs. Possible to develop shine.	Lustrous, with remarkable drapability. Possible snagging of floats.	Similar to satin. Can be made from staple yarns and Schreinerized for a lustrous finish.	Interesting texture. May have good strength, drapability, durability and resilience, depending on a number of factors such as the fiber, yarn twist, structure and compactness.
TYPICAL FABRICS	denim, drill, gabardine, tweed, houndstooth, herringbone	satin, slipper satin, crepe-back satin, duchesse satin	sateen	granite, moss crepe, sand crepe, wool crepe

225

TEXTILE

Fiber / Yarn / **Fabric** / Leather / Lace / Finishing / Fabric Pattern / Organic Textile / Fabric Selection Guide / Fabric Dictionary

BASIC FANCY WEAVES

NAME	FIGURE WEAVES		
PLAN VIEW	JACQUARD	TAPESTRY	PIQUÉ
		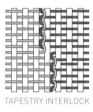 TAPESTRY INTERLOCK	CROSS SECTION 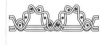 ⬜ weft yarn ● warp yarn
PHOTO / STRUCTURE			
	Possible to use any combination of weaves and patterns, as each warp is controlled individually with each pick passage.	A thick fabric with multi-colored, pictorial woven patterns, with the warp yarn controlling the color. Nowadays, it is mostly replaced by jacquard tapestry.	A fabric with pronounced ridges, known as wales or cords, which are upheld by floats on the back surface. In better quality pique textiles, 'stuffer yarns' are laid under the wales or cords to enhance the fullness. Cotton yarn is always used for pique weave.
APPEARANCE	Multi-colored and unlimited variety of intricate designs on all types of backgrounds.	Tapestry is a type of weft-faced weaving, with all warp threads concealed in the finished product, in comparison to cloth weaving where both the warp and weft threads can be seen.	The word 'piqué' originates from the French term for 'quilted', as the raised effect in piqué fabrics resembles those in quilts.
PROPERTIES	Attractive, good drapability and reasonable durability, which depends on the weave and yarn used.	Attractive yet bulky. Used as decorative textile art rather than in apparel.	Interesting finish and surface effects.
TYPICAL FABRICS	brocade, brocatelle, damask, matelassé, jacquard tapestry	jacquard tapestry	waved piqué, loose back piqué

SURFACE FIGURE WEAVES

PILE WEAVES

	DOBBY	SWIVEL	UNCUT PILE	CUT PILE
PLAN VIEW				

	DOBBY	SWIVEL	UNCUT PILE	CUT PILE
PHOTO / STRUCTURE	HUCKABACK Multiple types of interlacings. Could create geometric patterns.	DOTTED SWISS Surface of fabric is woven with small designs by insertion of extra weft yarns.	TERRY CLOTH An additional set of warps or wefts is woven over the ground yarns of plain or twill weave to create loops on the surface.	VELVET Similar to uncut pile but with the pile loops cut.
APPEARANCE	Decorative designs. Often with a ribbed effect, resulting in a textured surface.	Decorative, sometimes multi-colored designs. Extra yarns are used to form the design and are cut on the reverse side.	Yarns woven perpendicularly into the ground weave results in a three-dimensional effect in uncut pile fabrics.	Soft, brush-like texture. Sometimes with rows of cut pile in various lengths.
PROPERTIES	Attractive, and generally good body.	Attractive. Design yarns may roughen on the back and pull out.	Soft, warm, absorbent and resilient, with interesting texture and surface effects. Softness and absorbency are determined by the loops' compactness and the twist of pile yarn.	Soft, warm, absorbent and resilient, with interesting texture and surface effects. Softness and absorbency are determined by the loops' compactness and the twist of pile yarn.
TYPICAL FABRICS	huckaback, granite weave	dotted swiss	frieze, terry cloth	corduroy velvet, velveteen

TEXTILE

Fiber / Yarn / **Fabric** / Leather / Lace / Finishing / Fabric Pattern / Organic Textile / Fabric Selection Guide / Fabric Dictionary

GAUZE (LENO)	DOUBLE CLOTH	SLACK TENSION	TRIAXIAL
LENO WEAVE		SEERSUCKER	TRIAXIAL WEAVE
Pairs of warps are inter-twisted after each weft passes through.	Two units of separately woven fabrics are woven together using an extra set of yarns.	A variation of pile weave, slack tension fabric is made by releasing the tension from some warp yarns in the loom to create texture or pile.	Constructed from three yarns running in different angles.
An open mesh structure with securely held yarns. Variations include ribbed effects.	Different on both surfaces, may be reversible. Thick and heavy.	Crinkly stripes, piled surface.	Porous structure with a cane-like pattern.
Sheer, gauzy, lightweight yet durable.	Good strength and warmth. Possibly bulky.	Absorbent and non-wrinkling.	Good strength and stability. Limited stretch.
grenadine, marquisette	blanket cloth, coatings, upholstery	seersucker	industrial uses and home furnishings

KNIT

Knitting is a common type of textile and fabric production method using yarn. The two main types of knit fabrics are 'weft-knit' and 'warp-knit' fabrics. Warp-knitted textiles, such as tricot and Milanese, are resistant to runs and commonly used for lingerie. Weft-knit fabrics are more common and easier to produce, but are susceptible to unravelling (running) when cut, unless they are repaired.

PLAN VIEW

TECHNICAL FRONT

TECHNICAL BACK

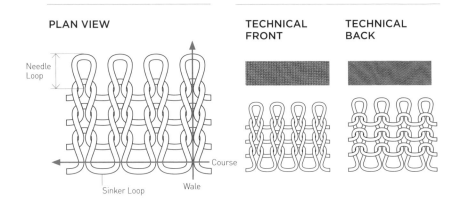

Needle Loop

Course

Sinker Loop

Wale

LATCH NEEDLE

LATCH NEEDLE MOVEMENT

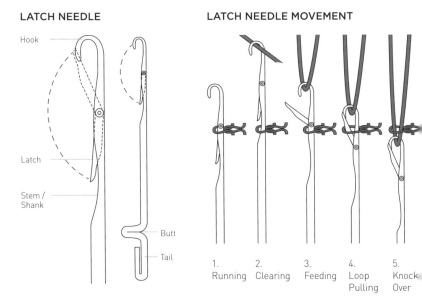

Hook

Latch

Stem / Shank

Butt

Tail

1. Running
2. Clearing
3. Feeding
4. Loop Pulling
5. Knock Over

TEXTILE

Fiber / Yarn / **Fabric** / Leather / Lace / Finishing / Fabric Pattern / Organic Textile / Fabric Selection Guide / Fabric Dictionary

BASIC LOOPS

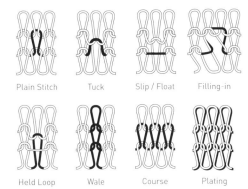

Plain Stitch   Tuck   Slip / Float   Filling-in

Held Loop   Wale   Course   Plating

KNIT SYMBOLS

+	selvage stitch
I or ☐	stockinette stitch
– or •	reverse stockinette stitch
୨ or ╱	twisted stockinette stitch
V	slip stitch knitwise
V̲ or I	slip stitch purlwise
O	yarn over
୪ or U	make one through back loop
୮ or V	increase 1 stitch- RS: knit into front and back of stitch; WS: purl into back and front of stitch
V	(k1, p1,k1) all in same stitch
V or ▼	multiple increase (refer to key)
⟋ or ◿	right-slanting decrease
⟍ or ◺	left-slanting decrease
⟋ or ◢	right-slanting double decrease
⟍ or ◣	left-slanting double decrease
⋀ or ▲	multiple decrease
–	bind off
■	no stitch
• or ⊙	knot or bobble (refer to key)
✕ or ⌐	right twist (2 sts)
✕ or ⌐	left twist (2 sts)
⋙ or ⟋⟋	cable 4 sts to right
⋙ or ⋙	cable 6 sts to left

NEEDLE SIZES

(mm)	US	UK	JP
2.0	0	14	
2.1			0
2.25	1	13	
2.4			1
2.5			
2.7			2
2.75	2	12	
3.0		11	3
3.25	3	10	
3.3			4
3.5	4		
3.6			5
3.75	5	9	
3.9			6
4.0	6	8	
4.2			7
4.5	7	7	8
4.8			9
5.0	8	6	
5.1			10
5.4			11
5.5	9	5	
5.7			12
6.0	10	4	13
6.3			14
6.5	10.5	3	
6.6			15
7.0		2	7mm
7.5		1	
8.0	11	0	8mm
9.0	13	00	9mm
10.0	15	000	10mm
12.0	17		
16.0	19		
19.0	35		
25.0	50		

BASIC WEFT KNITS

NAME	SINGLE JERSEY	PURL KNIT	1 × 1 RIB
STRUCTURE			
APPEARANCE	 FRONT　　BACK The simplest weft-knit structure, plain jersey fabric has flat, vertical lines on the front-facing surface and pronounced horizontal ribs on the reverse side.	 A simple purl fabric has the appearance of the back of jersey knit on both sides. They are produced on purl knit or links-and-links machines.	 1 × 1 rib has alternating wales knitted on both the front and back. The ribs usually close up, resulting in a double-faced fabric which has the same appearance on both surfaces.
PROPERTIES	Stretches both crosswise and lengthwise, but more in the crosswise direction. A less stable fabric, single jersey may unravel or ladder if the stitch breaks and curls when cut.	With similar appearances on both sides, purl knits stretch well in all directions but easily stretch out of shape. Thicker than jersey knits and resistant to curling at the edges. Slow production process.	Thicker and more elastic than jersey knits, 1x1 rib offers more stretch crosswise than lengthwise, and the edges do not curl. It is more expensive to produce.
TYPICAL USE	Used for sweaters, terry robes, T-shirts, dresses, men's underwear, women's hosiery and pantyhose. Also used for making fully fashioned garments.	Used for infant and children's clothing, sweaters and scarves.	Used for T-shirt collars, double knit jackets, knit beanies, men's socks and sometimes for the hem of sweaters.

TEXTILE

Fiber / Yarn / **Fabric** / Leather / Lace / Finishing / Fabric Pattern / Organic Textile / Fabric Selection Guide / Fabric Dictionary

2 × 2 RIB	INTERLOCK	SINGLE PIQUÉ	FRENCH TERRY

FRONT   BACK

2 × 2 rib has two alternating wales knitted on both the front and back.	Produced on a cylinder and dial circular weft knitting machine, where alternating long and short needles are positioned opposite to each other on the cylinder and dial.	Single piqué has an allover cellular, geometric textured surface, created by tuck loops and tuck stitches. Piqué means to pierce or to make a hole or opening.	A type of single jersey fabric. The technical face is basically jersey, while the technical back shows un-napped float stitches (loops).
Thicker and more elastic than 1 × 1 rib, 2 × 2 rib offers more stretch crosswise than lengthwise, and the edges do not curl.	Heavier and thicker than rib knits, interlock is a reversible fabric, does not curl at the edges, and offers good insulation. More expensive to produce.	The most productive amongst all types of piqué fabrics.	A light- to medium-weight fabric. The un-napped, looped side of French terry cloth is highly absorbent, as with regular terry cloth.
Used for cuffs and hems of sweaters.	Used for everyday garments such as dresses, skirts, blouses, T-shirts and outerwear.	Used on many polo shirts, ladies' dresses and other apparel.	More lightweight and with one smooth side, French terry cloth is suitable for garments, especially sportswear and beachwear.

BASIC WARP KNIT

NAME	SINGLE BAR CONSTRUCTIONS		
STRUCTURE	**PILLAR STITCH**	**HALF TRICOT**	**SINGLE ATLAS**
APPEARANCE			
	Also known as a chain stitch, a pillar stitch is a type of stitch construction in which both over and underlappings are performed across the same needle.	Also known as 1&1 closed lap / open lap, half tricot is the most basic type of warp knit construction. In the repeated two-course process, the guide bar feeds yarns on a needle in the first course, then moves sideways to feed yarns to the adjacent needle in the second course. The cycle is then repeated.	Created by the progressive lapping movement of the guide bar in the same direction for at least two consecutive courses, usually followed by identical lapping in the opposite direction.
PROPERTIES	Due to the absence of lateral connections with adjacent wales, pillar stitch offers only a link-up in the direction of the wales. It can only form a fabric by adding a weft yarn.	With very limited functions on its own, half tricot is however a popular combination for multi-guide bar structures. It is lightweight and sheer.	Changes in the lapping movement result in changes in the position of the overlaps and underlaps, thus creating diagonal stripes and causing differential light reflections.
TYPICAL USE	The most common use of the pillar stitch is for adding weft yarns to link up the loop chains. It can also be combined with multi-guide bar structures, such as Queen's cord.	Used for lining and lingerie	Used for creating fabrics with shadow stripes.

MULTI-BAR CONSTRUCTIONS

FULL TRICOT	SHARKSKIN	QUEEN'S CORD	RASCHEL

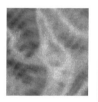   

Fine lengthwise ribs on one surface, and crosswise ribs on the reverse. Possible to produce complex patterns on some machines. Incorporating a weft insertion (extra crosswise-inserted yarn) will give the fabric added color or texture.	Sharkskin stitch has a longer underlap 4-5 / 1-0 on the back guide bar.	A stable fabric structure using the pillar stitch as the warp and long underlaps as the weft yarns.	Produced on a raschel-knitting machine, Raschel fabrics are diverse in nature and come in a wide variety. Interesting textures and surface designs can be created by incorporating conventional or novelty yarns. They can have a fine or lace-like open construction, complex patterns or even piled textures.
Offers some stretch lengthwise and almost no stretch crosswise. Normally soft and drapable. The cut edges tend to curl.	The longer lapping gives the sharkskin stitch a heavier weight and more dimensional stability.	Offers high dimensional stability comparable to woven fabrics.	Highly versatile, Raschel knits can be either stretchy or stable, single-faced or reversible, and cover a broad selection ranging from lofty open structures to dense and compact fabrics.
Traditionally used in lining and lingerie. Can also be used for blouses and dresses. It is crucial to assess the amount of stretch of the tricot fabric before garment production.	Used in fabrics which require high dimensional stability.	Used in fabrics which require high dimensional stability.	Can be used for almost all sorts of garments.

NONWOVEN FABRIC

Nonwoven fabrics are not constructed by weaving, knitting, or interlacing yarn, but by directly entangling separate fibers, filaments, molten plastic or plastic film together, mechanically, thermally, chemically, or by solvent treatment, creating a bonded sheet or web structure that is usually flat and porous.

NONWOVEN FABRIC CLASSIFICATION

STAPLE FIBER WEB COMPOSITION

CONTINUOUS FILAMENT WEB COMPOSITION

/ Dry-laid webs
/ Parallel-laid
/ Cross-laid
/ Random-laid
/ Composite webs

Wet-laid webs
(Modified paper)
(Apertured)

Foam

Film

Filaments

SPUNLAID

ADHESIVE BONDING

NEEDLE PUNCHING

STITCH BONDING

Needle Punching

Heat Pressure

Bi-component Filament

Self-Bonding

Spray

Base

Baseless

Fiber

Fiber / Yarn

Yarn

Total impregnation or link /nip

Powders

Spray

Foam

Fibers, threads or film

Print bonding

Spinlaced

Ultrasonic bonding

Thermal bonding

235

TEXTILE

Fiber / Yarn / **Fabric** / Leather / Lace / Finishing / Fabric Pattern / Organic Textile / Fabric Selection Guide / Fabric Dictionary

USES OF NONWOVEN FABRIC

MEDICAL

Surgical gowns

Surgical caps

Surgical drapes
and covers

Surgical masks

HYGIENE

Baby diapers /
nappies

Bandages /
wound dressings

Disposable bath /
face towels

Feminine
hygiene products

FILTERS

Tea bags /
coffee bags

Liquid cartridge
and bag filters

Gasoline, oil and air
filters; Including
HEPA filtration

Mineral
processing

GEOTEXTILES

Soil stabilizers
and roadway
underlayment

Drainage
systems

Frost protection

Agricultural
mulch

5.4 **LEATHER**

Leather is a type of material consisting of the skin of an animal made smooth and flexible by tanning, removing the hair, etc. It is a durable and flexible material with excellent resistance to abrasion and wind. Common leather sources are cattle, sheep, alligator, etc. Leather can be priced by number of pieces or by the subdivision of leather e.g. butt, bend, shoulder, head or belly. Products priced by piece rate have one price regardless of the sizes of the products. Products priced by the subdivision are generally priced by the yard or square foot and therefore the price varies according to the sizes of the products.

SUBDIVISIONS OF LEATHER

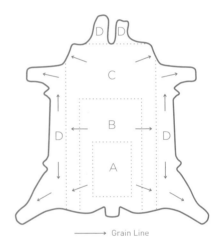

A . Butt

Best Value
13% of the hide

B . Bend

Good Value
30% of the hide

C . Shoulder

Fair Value
32% of the hide

D . Head, Belly

Poor Value
25% of the hide

Grain Line

THICKNESS SYSTEM CONVERSION

Ounces		Thickness	Ounces		Thickness
1		0.4 mm	9		3.6 mm
2		0.8 mm	10		4.0 mm
3		1.2 mm	11		4.4 mm
4		1.6 mm	12		4.8 mm
5		2.0 mm	13		5.2 mm
6		2.4 mm	14		5.6 mm
7		2.8 mm	15		6.0 mm
8		3.2 mm			

237

TEXTILE

Fiber / Yarn / Fabric / **Leather** / Lace / Finishing / Fabric Pattern / Organic Textile / Fabric Selection Guide / Fabric Dictionary

LEATHER IDENTIFICATION

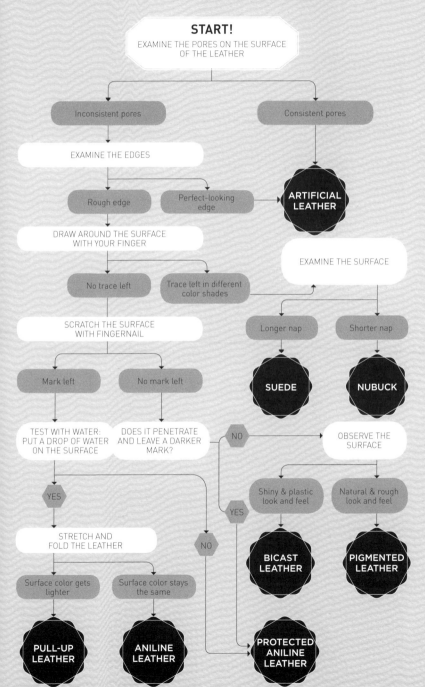

START!
EXAMINE THE PORES ON THE SURFACE OF THE LEATHER

Inconsistent pores

Consistent pores

EXAMINE THE EDGES

Rough edge

Perfect-looking edge

ARTIFICIAL LEATHER

DRAW AROUND THE SURFACE WITH YOUR FINGER

EXAMINE THE SURFACE

No trace left

Trace left in different color shades

Longer nap

Shorter nap

SCRATCH THE SURFACE WITH FINGERNAIL

SUEDE

NUBUCK

Mark left

No mark left

TEST WITH WATER: PUT A DROP OF WATER ON THE SURFACE

DOES IT PENETRATE AND LEAVE A DARKER MARK?

NO

OBSERVE THE SURFACE

YES

Shiny & plastic look and feel

Natural & rough look and feel

YES

STRETCH AND FOLD THE LEATHER

NO

BICAST LEATHER

PIGMENTED LEATHER

Surface color gets lighter

Surface color stays the same

PULL-UP LEATHER

ANILINE LEATHER

PROTECTED ANILINE LEATHER

LEATHER TYPES

Cattle

Most leather is made of cattle skin, structure varies across the whole hide, strong.

Calf

Slightly rubbery, fine grain, little variation across the skin.

Buffalo

Strong, tough, rubbery feel, pebbly appearance, thick.

Goat

Strong, thin, fine grain, regular pattern, papery feel.

Sheep

Good heat insulation. Thin, soft, loose fibrous structure. Loose grain surface and light substance with soft feel, very porous. Low durability.

Lamb

The softest, thinnest, most supple type of skin. Buttery texture and finely grained. Elastic, very form-fitting, stretches well and tends to reshape after wearing.

Deer

Tough, soft, supple, very stretchy. Washable and abrasion resistant.

Elk

Similar to deerskin except very heavy and much thicker.

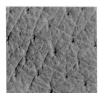

Pigskin

High breathability. Soft, thin, supple, durable, relatively tough with tight grain. Common hide for suede.

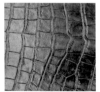

Alligator

Thick in the bend and thin in the belly and limbs. Scaly, supple (belly), tough, durable.

Snake

Great variation depending on the type of snake, distinctive pattern, lightweight, strong, papery feel.

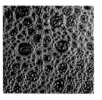

Frog / Toad

Lightweight, thin, strong, great variation depending on the type of the species.

239

TEXTILE

Fiber / Yarn / Fabric / **Leather** / Lace / Finishing / Fabric Pattern / Organic Textile / Fabric Selection Guide / Fabric Dictionary

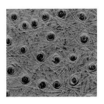

Ostrich

One of the finest and most durable types of skins in the world. Unique bumpy texture. Flexible, pliable, durable and soft, very strong.

Kangaroo

Very strong (10 times the tensile strength of cowhide and is 50% stronger than goatskin), thin, lightweight, uniform fiber structure.

Salmon

Fine scales, pliable, strong and elegant looking. The most popular fish leather.

Perch

Sourced from the Nile. Thick, large and soft round scales.

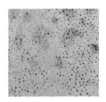

Wolffish

Smooth skin, scaleless. Easily recognizable thanks to its dark spots and 'stripes' which are due to the friction of marine rocks.

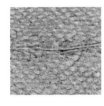

Cod

Its skin has finer scales than salmon, but its texture is more varied, sometimes smooth and sometimes rough.

Eel

Very smooth in touch with an elegant horizontal pinstripe-like pattern. Lightweight, supple, incredibly strong. Sewn together to create a leather panel.

Tilapia

Compared with salmon skin, the pattern of tilapia leather is more beautiful, but the skins are smaller in size.

Stingray

Distinctive pattern. Highly durable (25 times more durable than cowhide) and has a unique supple texture.

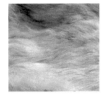

Rabbit

Small in size, thin and fragile.

Lizard

Strong, lightweight, papery feel and thin.

Horse

Tough, thin, non-uniform quality, stretches well, Commonly used for making shoes.

5.5 **LACE**

Made of yarn or thread, lace is a delicate handmade or machine-produced fabric with an open web-like pattern. It was originally made from linen, silk, gold or silver threads. Today it is more often produced using cotton thread, though it is still available in linen and silk thread versions. Synthetic fibers may be used in manufactured lace.

A number of factors determine the quality of lace, including the fineness of yarns, number of yarns per square inch, density of background net, and the intricacy of the pattern or design.

CLASSIFICATION OF LACE

HANDMADE LACE

MACHINE-MADE LACE

NEEDLE POINT LACE	BOBBIN LACE	CROCHETED LACE	TAPE LACE
Alencon	Torchon	Hairpin	Battenberg
Point de gaze	Blonde	Filet crochet	Mezzopunto
Filet / Lacis	Chantilly	Broomstick lace	Princess
Carrick-macross	Lillie	Irish crochet & more	Renaissance
Point de Venise	Valenciennes		Romanian point
Point de France	Antwerp		Branscombe & more
Buratto	Mechlin		
Teneriffe & more	Maltese		
	Honiton		
	Bruges		
	Brussels & more		

LEAVERS LACE	RASCHEL KNIT LACE	CHEMICAL LACE

The lace machine was developed to speed up the lace making process. In 1818, John Leavers developed a machine that made patterns and the background net simultaneously. A card system, similar to the technique used on card jacquard looms, made it possible to produce intricate designs with the leaver machine.

The Leavers machine consists of warp yarns and oscillating bobbins that are set in frames called carriages. The carriages move back and forth with the bobbins swinging around the warp to form a pattern. Leavers lace is fairly expensive, depending on the quality of yarns used and the intricacy of the design.

Raschel knitting machines use the warp knitting technique to make patterned lace that looks similar to Leavers lace. Raschel lace can be made at much higher speeds and thus is less expensive to produce.

COMMON HANDMADE LACE

Alençon Needle Lace

Delicate, durable, needlepoint lace with solid designs outlined in cord on a sheer net ground. Traditionally handmade in Alençon, France, it nowadays has machine-made imitations with cords run in by hand.

Filet / Lacis Needle Lace

A type of handmade lace with a grid-like open mesh foundation. Patterns are created by filling selected squares on the knotted mesh ground using darning stitches.

Brussels Point de Gaze Needle Lace

Traditionally crafted with either needlepoint or pillow designs surrounded by a bobbin-made ground. Nowadays, the lace designs are made separately and appliquéd on a machine-made net ground.

Carrickmacross Needle Lace

Irish needlepoint lace using appliqué or guipure techniques. Created by layering sheer fabric with designs onto a plain, machine-made net, finished with buttonhole- or chain-stitch and trimming away material around the design.

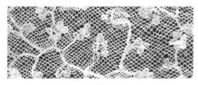

Antwerp Bobbin Lace

Rare bobbin lace designed with flower motifs in baskets or pots. Formerly popular amongst Antwerp women for trimming caps.

Valenciennes Bobbin Lace

A fine bobbin lace worked in one single piece, forming both the design and ground with the same thread. Designs of florals and trailing patterns are fashioned on open, regular mesh, without any raised work or cordonnet.

Chantilly Bobbin Lace

A type of handmade bobbin lace which can be closely imitated by machines. The design is outlined by a cordonnet of thin, silky threads on a fine ground.

Honiton Appliqué Bobbin Lace

A usually machine-made lace, with motifs separately made and sewn to a net ground.

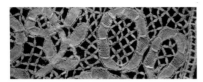

Honiton Guipure Bobbin Lace

Resembles Honiton appliqué bobbin lace, but with round, heavy motifs made up of fine braids, linked by needle-made braids.

Lille Bobbin Lace

Fine bobbin lace such as Mechlin, with outlined patterns in heavy, flat cordonnet. Sometimes dotted.

Maltese Bobbin Lace

Traditionally similar to the designs of Mechlin lace and Val lace. The modern-day version is a guipure lace with simple, geometric designs, incorporating the Maltese cross and dots.

Mechlin Bobbin Lace

Filmy bobbin lace on a hexagonal mesh net ground. The intricately woven design, traditionally of ornaments and flowers, is outlined with a flat, shiny cordonnet.

Torchon Bobbin Lace

Also known as beggar's lace or peasant lace, it is a coarse and durable bobbin lace made from wither linen or cotton thread.

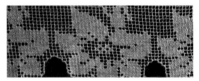

Filet Crochet

Uses only two crochet stitches - the chain stitch and the double crochet stitch - resulting in a grid-like pattern.

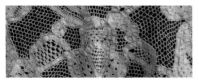

Battenberg Tape Lace

Coarse lace with designs created by bringing together linen braid or tape and linen thread. Can be both handmade and machine-made.

Bruges Tape Lace

Fine guipure tape lace produced with bobbins. Its fine woven version is used for dresses, while the coarse woven counterpart is used for curtains and table linen finishing.

TEXTILE

Fiber / Yarn / Fabric / Leather / **Lace** / Finishing / Fabric Pattern / Organic Textile / Fabric Selection Guide / Fabric Dictionary

COMMON MACHINE-MADE LACE

Leavers Lace

The intertwined lace structure is created on a Leavers machine with over 10,000 yarns that are set to make hoops with bobbins. The design is marked on a punching card called a Jacquard Card, which gives the machine instructions for moving the yarns in left-right directions to weave out the desired pattern.

Raschel Lace

Raschel lace has a similar appearance to Leavers lace, but the Raschel lace machine is actually a type of knitting machine, which creates designs and motifs in a warp-knit structure. The structure is entirely different from Leavers lace even when the same yarn is used. The Jacquard Card method and Chain Drum method are adopted to reflect the design and to feed it through the machine.

Chemical Lace

Chemical lace (also known as Schiffli lace) is a type of machine-made lace. The designed pattern is embroidered on a chemically-treated, soluble fabric, which is then immersed in a solution that completely dissolves the soluble fabric and leaves only the embroidered lace intact.

5.6 **FINISHINGS**
DYEING & PRINTING

In textile production, finishings refer to the treatments that convert greige goods (woven or knit fabrics fresh off the loom. See: Glossary) into a usable material for garment production. More specifically, it includes all processes carried out after dyeing the yarn or textile, which may involve improving the look, handfeel or performance of the finished fabric or garment. The exact meaning varies depending on the context.

Finishing processes may be performed both pre- and post-fabric production. Techniques such as bleaching and dyeing are carried out on the yarn before weaving, while other finishing processes are applied on woven or knitted grey cloths directly after they are taken off the loom (loom state textiles). Finishing techniques have been evolving throughout the history of textile production. Certain types, such as fulling, have been adopted in hand-weaving for centuries, while other more modern procedures, such as mercerization, were invented during the Industrial Revolution.

**DIFFERENT TYPES OF
TEXTILE FINISHINGS**

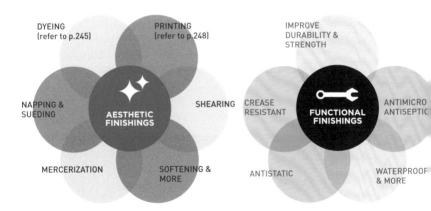

DYEING
(refer to p.245)

PRINTING
(refer to p.248)

IMPROVE
DURABILITY &
STRENGTH

NAPPING &
SUEDING

**AESTHETIC
FINISHINGS**

SHEARING

CREASE
RESISTANT

**FUNCTIONAL
FINISHINGS**

ANTIMICRO
ANTISEPTIC

MERCERIZATION

SOFTENING &
MORE

ANTISTATIC

WATERPROOF
& MORE

TEXTILE

Fiber / Yarn / Fabric / Leather / Lace / **Finishing** / Fabric Pattern / Organic Textile / Fabric Selection Guide / Fabric Dictionary

DYEING

Dyeing refers to the process of giving color to textile products, including fibers, yarns and fabrics. It is usually done in a special solution that contains the dye of the desired color and certain chemical materials, which create an uncut chemical bond between the dye molecules and fiber molecules once the dyeing process is complete. Dyeing has two key determining factors: temperature and time control. The two main types of dye are natural and synthetic.

STAGES OF DYEING

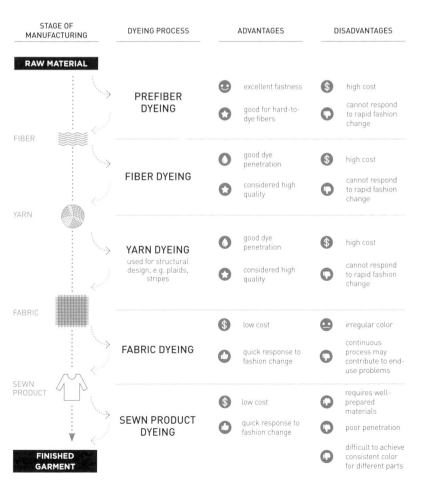

STAGE OF MANUFACTURING	DYEING PROCESS	ADVANTAGES	DISADVANTAGES
RAW MATERIAL			
	PREFIBER DYEING	excellent fastness / good for hard-to-dye fibers	high cost / cannot respond to rapid fashion change
FIBER	FIBER DYEING	good dye penetration / considered high quality	high cost / cannot respond to rapid fashion change
YARN	YARN DYEING used for structural design, e.g. plaids, stripes	good dye penetration / considered high quality	high cost / cannot respond to rapid fashion change
FABRIC	FABRIC DYEING	low cost / quick response to fashion change	irregular color / continuous process may contribute to end-use problems
SEWN PRODUCT	SEWN PRODUCT DYEING	low cost / quick response to fashion change	requires well-prepared materials / poor penetration / difficult to achieve consistent color for different parts
FINISHED GARMENT			

MAJOR DYE CLASSES

DYE CLASS	FIBER TYPE	DESCRIPTION	END-USES
DIRECT	CELLULOSIC	complete shade range; simple application; colors duller than basic or acid dyes	low quality apparel fabrics, lining, curtains
REACTIVE	CELLULOSIC PROTEIN	chemically reacts with the fiber forming covalent bonds; resulting in high color fastness; brilliant shades; higher cost	curtains, furnishings, apparel fabrics, toweling, sewing threads
VAT	CELLULOSIC	synthetic indigo invented in 1879; insoluble in water; best all-around fastness properties; expensive; incomplete shade range	high quality curtains, furnishing, shirts, towels, sewing threads
SULFUR	CELLULOSIC	after-treatment is required to prevent the fiber from becoming tender after oxidation of the sulfur; not bright enough in color shades; lower cost	primarily for cotton fabrics, most widely used black dye
AZOIC	CELLULOSIC	water-insoluble; complete shade range; provides an economical way to obtain certain shades, especially red shades	primarily for cotton fabrics
ACID	PROTEIN SYNTHETIC	water-soluble; applies to the fiber directly from solutions containing an acid (acetic, formic or sulfuric acid); complete color range; easy application	carpet yarns, dresses, suitings, overcoats, knitting yarns
MORDANT	PROTEIN	addition of chrome in the dyebath required; dull but has a wide range of color; best all-round fastness properties on wool	carpet yarns, dresses, suitings, overcoats, knitting yarn
BASIC	SYNTHETIC	fast dyeing and can easily be applied to acrylic fiber; complete and brilliant color range	furnishings, apparel fabrics
DISPERSE	SYNTHETIC	developed for acetate fiber (also known as acetate dyes); water-insoluble, good shade range	apparel fabrics, bed sheets, carpets

FASTNESS PROPERTIES

WASHING	CROCKING	LIGHT	PERSPIRATION	DRY CLEANING
		poor on nylon		
	depends on dye type & depth of shade			
sensitive to chlorine bleach	depends on shade, depth & after-treatment	poor to fair for yellows and browns; excellent for darker colors		
	depends on dyeing technique and after-treatment	depends on type, shade and depth		
		generally very good; range from poor to excellent		
		depends on depth of shade and dyeing method		
better on polyesters				

PRINTING

Textile printing refers to the process of adding colored, sharply defined patterns or designs to either the whole or certain parts of a fabric. It is related to dyeing, but dyeing involves uniformly covering the fabric with one color. The color in properly printed fabrics is bonded with the fiber, and is wash- and friction-resistant.

CLASSIFICATION OF PRINTING

RESIST PRINTING	DISCHARGE PRINTING	DIRECT PRINTING*	OTHERS
Batik	White Discharge Printing	Block Printing	Flocking
Tie-Dyeing	Color Discharge Printing	Engraved Roller Printing	Yarn Printing
Ikat		Flat-Bed Screen Printing	Warp Printing
Plangi		Rotary Screen Printing	Hank Printing
Spray Painting		Transfer Printing (Dry)	
		Transfer Printing (Wet)	
		Digital Printing	

* Refer to the opposite page

PROCESS OF DIFFERENT DIRECT PRINTING METHODS

BLOCK PRINTING

Design   Block preparation   Printing by hand

ENGRAVED ROLLER PRINTING

Design   Roller preparation   Printing

FLAT-BED SCREEN PRINTING

Design   Screen preparation   Printing

ROTARY SCREEN PRINTING

Design   Screen preparation   Printing

TRANSFER PRINTING (DRY)

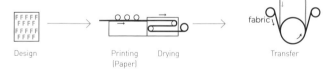

Design   Printing   Drying   Transfer
                  (Paper)

TRANSFER PRINTING (WET)

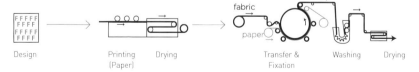

Design   Printing   Drying   Transfer &   Washing   Drying
                  (Paper)   Fixation

DIGITAL PRINTING

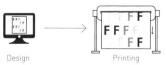

Design   Printing

COMPARISON OF DIFFERENT DIRECT PRINTING METHODS

PRINTING METHOD	PRODUCTIVITY	CAPITAL COST	OPERATIVE SKILL LEVEL
BLOCK PRINTING	↑ (low)	$$$	👤👤👤👤
ENGRAVED ROLLER PRINTING	↑ (high)	$$$	👤👤👤👤
FLAT-BED SCREEN PRINTING	↑ (high)	$$$	👤👤👤
ROTARY SCREEN PRINTING	↑ (high)	$	👤👤👤
TRANSFER PRINTING (DRY)	↑ (low)	$	👤👤
TRANSFER PRINTING (WET)	↑ (low)	$$	👤👤
DIGITAL PRINTING	↑ (low)	$$$$	👤

| DESIGN LIMITATIONS | | FABRIC LIMITATIONS | | |
COMPLEXITY	PATTERN REPEAT SIZE	FABRIC WIDTH	MATERIAL	DYE UTILIZATION
★★ Depends on the skills of the block maker	★ Limited	★★★★★ Wide width possible	★★★★★ Unlimited	★★★★★ Bright color
★★★★★ Very fine details & tone effects	★★ Limited (Max. 41 cm)	★★★ Limited	★★★★★ Unlimited	★★★★ Duller colors than screen print
★★★★ Fine details	★★★★★ High	★★★★★ Wide width possible	★★★★★ Unlimited	★★★★★ Bright color
★★★★ Fine details	★★★ Limited (Max. 100 cm)	★★★★★ Wide width possible	★★★★★ Unlimited	★★★★★ Bright color
★★★★★ Unlimited design	★★★ Depends on the size of paper	★★★★★ Wide width possible	★★★ Better on synthetic fabrics	★★★ 100% color saturation cannot be achieved
★★★★★ Unlimited design	★★★ Depends on the size of paper	★★★★★ Wide width possible	★★★ Better on synthetic fabrics	★★★ 100% color saturation cannot be achieved
★★★★★ Unlimited design	★★★★ High (depends on the width of the printer)	★★★★★ Wide width possible	★★★ Better on synthetic fabrics	★★★ 100% color saturation cannot be achieved

5.7 **FABRIC PATTERNS**

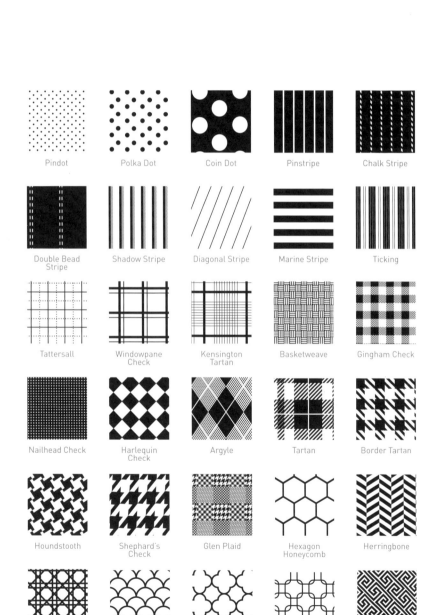

Pindot

Polka Dot

Coin Dot

Pinstripe

Chalk Stripe

Double Bead Stripe

Shadow Stripe

Diagonal Stripe

Marine Stripe

Ticking

Tattersall

Windowpane Check

Kensington Tartan

Basketweave

Gingham Check

Nailhead Check

Harlequin Check

Argyle

Tartan

Border Tartan

Houndstooth

Shephard's Check

Glen Plaid

Hexagon Honeycomb

Herringbone

Caning

Scale

Quatrefoil

Trellis

Fret

TEXTILE

Fiber / Yarn / Fabric / Leather / Lace / Finishing / **Fabric Pattern** / Organic Textile / Fabric Selection Guide / Fabric Dictionary

Geometric

Zigzag /
Chevron

Ogee

Spiral

Brick Path

Fleur de Lis

Cheetah

Zebra

Giraffe

Leopard

Tiger

Peacock

Paisley

William Morris

Damask

Vintage Floral

Toile de Jouy

Ditsy

Retro

Op Art

Abstract

Art Nouveau

Camouflage

Fair Isle

Tropical

Ikat

Chinese

Indian

African

Arabic

5.8 **ORGANIC TEXTILE**

With an exceptionally high pollutant discharge level, the textile industry is amongst one of the most polluting industries in the world. According to surveys, textile waste consumes nearly five percent of all landfill space, while textile treatments and dyeing contribute to 20 percent of all fresh water pollution.

Nowadays, consumers have become more aware of environmental issues and seek eco-friendliness in apparel products. In order to minimize environmental degradation at every possible stage, textile and garment manufacturers are encouraged to re-examine the life cycle of their products. Various organic textile labels offer user-friendly guidelines for consumers to examine apparel products based on a benchmarked system.

WHY DO WE NEED ORGANIC CLOTHING?

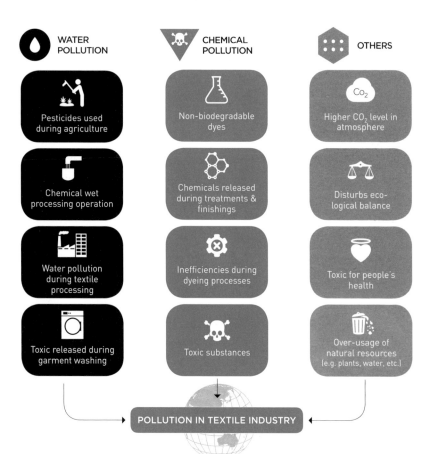

ORGANIC TEXTILE LABELS

The Global Organic Textile Standard (GOTS)
www.global-standard.org

Aims at unifying the various existing standards and draft standards in the field of eco textile processing, and to define world-wide recognized requirements that ensure the organic status of textiles, from harvesting raw materials, through environmental and social manufacturing responsible up to labeling, in order to provide a credible assurance to end consumers.

Organic Content Standard (OCS)
www.textileexchange.org

A voluntary chain of custody standard that provides companies with a tool for third-party verification that a final product contains the accurate amount of a given organically grown material. Each organization along the supply chain must take sufficient steps to ensure the integrity and identity of the organic material input. It does not address the use of chemicals or any social or environmental aspects of production beyond the integrity of the organic material.

International Association of Natural Textile Industry (IVN)
IVN Certified Best
www.naturtextil.com

Aside from ecological production processes and premiums, it also requires low-pollutant, environmentally-friendly qualities, and humane production conditions of the textiles. A further prerequisite is the use of 100% certified organic fibers. The requirement of Naturtextil label is even stricter than the GOTS label.

International Association of Natural Textile Industry (IVN)
IVN Natural Leather Standard
www.naturtextil.com

Establishes the requirements for the production of high quality leathers, with 'high quality' benchmarked in terms of technical, ecological and human health parameters.

Oeko-Tex Standard 100
www.oeko-tex.com

A global uniform testing and certification system for raw materials, intermediate and end product textiles at all stages of production. The certification covers multiple human-ecological attributes, including harmful substances which are prohibited or regulated by law, chemicals which are known to be harmful to health, but are not officially forbidden, and parameters which are included as a precautionary measure to safeguard health.

Bluesign Standard
www.bluesign.com

Instead of focusing on finished product testing, the bluesign standard analyzes all input streams – from raw materials to chemical components, to resources – with a sophisticated 'Input Stream Management' process. All components are assessed based on their ecotoxicological impact prior to production. Potentially harmful substances can thus be eliminated before production begins.

Cradle to Cradle Certified Product Standard
www.c2ccertified.org

This certificate guides designers and manufacturers through a continual improvement process that looks at a product through five quality categories - material health, material reutilization, renewable energy and carbon management, water stewardship, and social fairness.

MADE-BY
www.made-by.org

An umbrella label used by fashion brands and retailers to show consumers that their clothes are produced in a sustainable manner. The brands affiliated to MADE-BY use organic cotton and work with sewing factories that have a social code of conduct.
The MADE-BY brands can be identified by means of a blue button, which indicates that the brand produces its collection in a people- and environment-friendly manner.

5.9 SUGGESTED GUIDE FOR FABRIC SELECTION

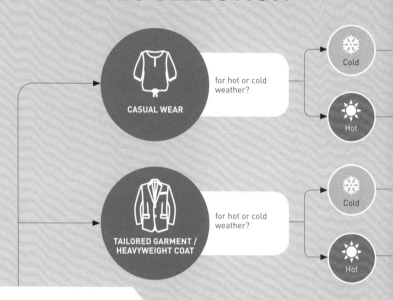

CASUAL WEAR — for hot or cold weather? — Cold / Hot

TAILORED GARMENT / HEAVYWEIGHT COAT — for hot or cold weather? — Cold / Hot

START!
WHAT TYPE OF GARMENT DO YOU WANT TO MAKE?

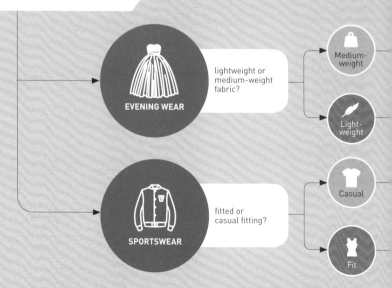

EVENING WEAR — lightweight or medium-weight fabric? — Medium-weight / Light-weight

SPORTSWEAR — fitted or casual fitting? — Casual / Fit

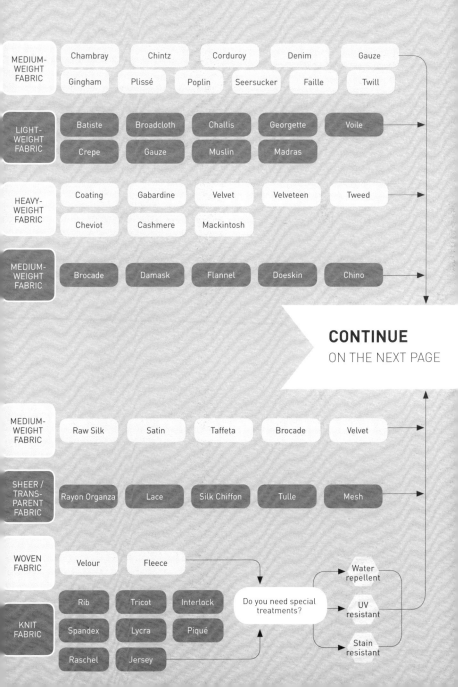

| MEDIUM-WEIGHT FABRIC | Chambray | Chintz | Corduroy | Denim | Gauze |
| | Gingham | Plissé | Poplin | Seersucker | Faille | Twill |

| LIGHT-WEIGHT FABRIC | Batiste | Broadcloth | Challis | Georgette | Voile |
| | Crepe | Gauze | Muslin | Madras |

| HEAVY-WEIGHT FABRIC | Coating | Gabardine | Velvet | Velveteen | Tweed |
| | Cheviot | Cashmere | Mackintosh |

| MEDIUM-WEIGHT FABRIC | Brocade | Damask | Flannel | Doeskin | Chino |

CONTINUE
ON THE NEXT PAGE

| MEDIUM-WEIGHT FABRIC | Raw Silk | Satin | Taffeta | Brocade | Velvet |

| SHEER / TRANSPARENT FABRIC | Rayon Organza | Lace | Silk Chiffon | Tulle | Mesh |

| WOVEN FABRIC | Velour | Fleece |

Do you need special treatments?

Water repellent

UV resistant

Stain resistant

KNIT FABRIC	Rib	Tricot	Interlock
	Spandex	Lycra	Piqué
	Raschel	Jersey

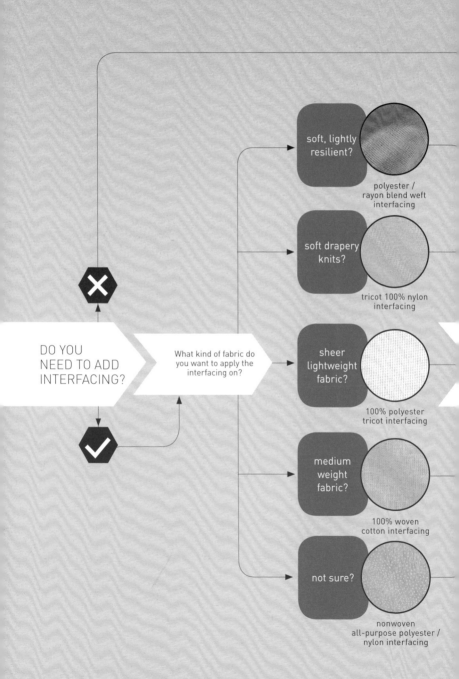

DO YOU
NEED TO ADD
INTERFACING?

What kind of fabric do you want to apply the interfacing on?

soft, lightly resilient?

polyester /
rayon blend weft
interfacing

soft drapery knits?

tricot 100% nylon
interfacing

sheer lightweight fabric?

100% polyester
tricot interfacing

medium weight fabric?

100% woven
cotton interfacing

not sure?

nonwoven
all-purpose polyester /
nylon interfacing

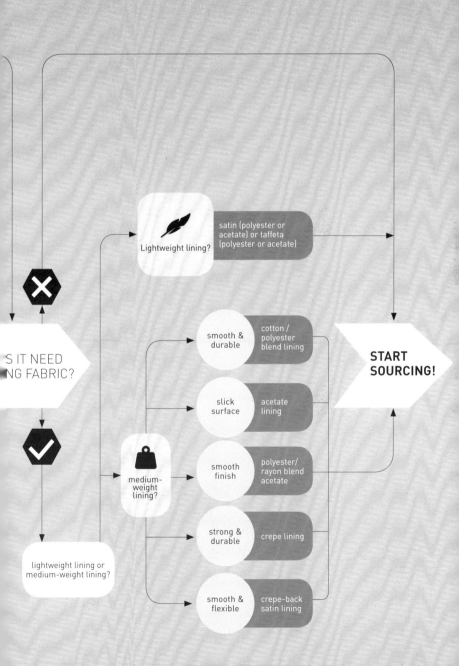

Lightweight lining?

satin (polyester or acetate) or taffeta (polyester or acetate)

IS IT NEED ING FABRIC?

lightweight lining or medium-weight lining?

medium-weight lining?

smooth & durable — cotton / polyester blend lining

slick surface — acetate lining

smooth finish — polyester/ rayon blend acetate

strong & durable — crepe lining

smooth & flexible — crepe-back satin lining

START SOURCING!

5.10 **FABRIC DICTIONARY**

Acrylic / warm, light, wool-like synthetic fabric

Aertex / trademark for a loosely woven cotton fabric that is used to make shirts and underwear

Alpaca / thin glossy fabric made of the wool of an alpaca, or rayon, or cotton imitation

Baize / bright green fabric napped to resemble felt

Basket Weave / cloth woven of two or more threads interlaced to form the weave of a basket

Batik / dyed fabric; a removable wax is used where the dye is not wanted; thin plain-weave cotton or linen fabric; used for shirts or dresses

Batiste / the material with which belts are made

Belting / fabric of uneven yarn that has an uneven knobby effect

Boucle / closely woven silk or synthetic fabric with a narrow crosswise rib

Broadcloth / densely textured woolen fabric with a lustrous finish

Brocade / thick heavy expensive material with a raised pattern

Buckram / coarse cotton fabric stiffened with glue; used to stiffen clothing and bookbinding

Bunting / loosely woven fabric used for flags, etc.

Calico / plain unbleached weave fabric

Cambric / finely woven white linen

Camel hair / soft tan cloth made with the hair of a camel

Camlet / fabric of Asian origin; originally made of silk and camel's hair

Camouflage / fabric dyed with splotches of green, brown, black and tan to make the wearer hard to distinguish from the background

Canopy / the umbrella-like part of a parachute that fills with air

Canvas / heavy closely woven fabric

Cashmere / soft fabric made of the wool of the cashmere goat

Cerecloth / waterproof waxed cloth once used as a shroud

Challis / soft lightweight fabric (usually printed)

Chambray / lightweight fabric woven with white threads across a colored warp

Chenille / heavy fabric woven with chenille cord

Chiffon / sheer fabric of silk or rayon

Chino / coarse twilled cotton fabric used for uniforms

Chintz / brightly printed and glazed cotton fabric

Coating / heavy fabric suitable for coats

Corduroy / cut pile fabric with vertical ribs; usually made of cotton

Cotton / fabric woven from cotton fibers

Canton Flannel / stout cotton fabric with nap on only one side

Crepe / soft thin light fabric with a crinkled surface

Cretonne / unglazed heavy fabric; brightly printed

Crinoline / stiff coarse fabric used to stiffen hats or clothing

Damask / fabric of linen, cotton, silk or wool with a reversible pattern woven into it

Denim / coarse durable twill-weave cotton fabric

Diamante / fabric covered with glittering ornaments such as rhinestones or sequins

Diaper / cotton or linen fabric with a distinctive woven pattern of small repeated figures

Dimity / strong cotton fabric with a raised pattern; used for bedcovers and curtains

Doeskin / fine smooth soft woolen fabric

Drapery / cloth gracefully draped and arranged in loose folds

Duck / heavy cotton fabric of plain weave; used for clothing and tents

Duffel / coarse heavy woolen fabric

Elastic / elastic fabric made of yarns containing an elastic material

Etamine / soft cotton with an open mesh; used for curtains or clothing etc.

Faille / ribbed woven fabric of silk or rayon or cotton

Felt / fabric made of compressed matted animal fibers

Flannel / soft light woolen fabric; used for clothing

Flannelette / cotton fabric imitating flannel

Fleece / soft bulky fabric with deep pile; used chiefly for clothing

Foulard / light plain-weave or twill-weave silk or silk-like fabric (usually with a printed design)

Frieze / heavy woolen fabric with a long nap

Fustian / strong cotton and linen fabric with a slight nap

Gabardine / firm durable fabric with a twill weave

Georgette / thin silk dress material

Gingham / clothing fabric in a plaid weave

Grogram / coarse fabric of silk mixed with wool or mohair and often stiffened with gum

Grosgrain / silk or silk-like fabric with crosswise ribs

Haircloth / cloth woven from horsehair or camel hair; used for upholstery or stiffening in garments

Herringbone / twilled fabric with a herringbone pattern

Homespun / rough loosely woven fabric made with homespun yarn

Hopsacking / loosely woven coarse fabric of cotton or linen

Horsehair / fabric made from horsehair fibers; used for upholstery

Khaki / sturdy twilled cloth of a yellowish brown color used especially for military uniforms

Knit / fabric made by knitting

Lace / delicate decorative fabric woven in an open web of symmetrical patterns

Lame / fabric interwoven with metallic threads

Leatherette / fabric made to look like leather

Linen / fabric woven with fibers from the flax plant

Linsey-Woolsey / rough fabric of linen warp and woolen weft

Lint / cotton or linen fabric with the nap raised on one side; used to dress wounds

Lisle / fabric woven with lisle thread

Mackinaw / heavy woolen cloth heavily napped

261

TEXTILE

Fiber / Yarn / Fabric / Leather / Lace / Finishing / Fabric Pattern / Organic Textile / Fabric Selection Guide / **Fabric Dictionary**

	and felted, often with a plaid design
Mackintosh	/ lightweight waterproof (usually rubberized) fabric
Madras	/ light patterned cotton cloth
Marseille	/ strong cotton fabric with a raised pattern; used for bedspreads
Mohair	/ fabric made with yarn from the silky hair of the Angora goat
Moire	/ silk fabric with a wavy surface pattern
Moleskin	/ durable cotton fabric with a velvety nap
Monk's Cloth	/ heavy cloth in basketweave
Moquette	/ thick velvety synthetic fabric used for carpets and soft upholstery
Moreen	/ heavy fabric of wool (or cotton) used especially in upholstery
Motley	/ multi-colored woolen fabric woven of mixed threads in the 14th to 17th centuries in England
Muslin	/ plain-woven cotton fabric
Nankeen	/ durable fabric formerly loomed by hand in China from natural cotton having a yellowish color
Net, Mesh	/ an open fabric woven together at regular intervals
Ninon	/ fine strong sheer silky fabric made of silk or rayon or nylon
Nylon	/ synthetic fabric
Oilcloth	/ cloth treated on one side with a drying oil or synthetic resin
Olive Drab	/ cloth of an olive-brown color used for military uniforms
Organza	/ fabric made of silk or a silk-like fabric that resembles organdy
Paisley	/ soft wool fabric with a colorful swirled pattern of curved shapes
Panting	/ any fabric used to make trousers
Percale	/ fine closely woven cotton fabric
Pilot Cloth	/ thick blue cloth used to make overcoats and coats for sailors etc.
Pina Cloth	/ fine cloth made from pineapple fibers
Pique	/ tightly woven fabric with raised cords
Plush	/ fabric with a nap that is longer and softer than velvet
Polyester	/ any of a large class of synthetic fabrics
Pongee	/ soft thin cloth woven from raw silk (or an imitation)
Poplin	/ lightweight plain-woven fabric with a corded surface
Print	/ fabric with a dyed pattern pressed onto it (usually by engraved rollers)
Quilting	/ material used for making a quilt, or fabric with such patterned stitching
Rayon	/ synthetic silk-like fabric
Sackcloth	/ coarse cloth resembling sacking
Sacking	/ coarse fabric used for bags or sacks
Sailcloth	/ strong fabric (such as cotton canvas) used for making tents and sails
Samite	/ heavy silk fabric (often woven with silver or gold threads); used to make clothing in the Middle Ages
Sateen	/ cotton fabric with a satiny finish
Satin	/ smooth fabric of silk or rayon; has a glossy face and a dull back
Screening	/ fabric of metal or plastic mesh
Scrim	/ firm open-weave fabric used for a curtain in the theater
Seersucker	/ light puckered fabric (usually

	striped)
Serge	/ twilled woolen fabric
Shag	/ fabric with long coarse nap
Shantung	/ heavy silk fabric with a rough surface (or a cotton imitation)
Sharkskin	/ smooth crisp fabric
Sheeting	/ fabric from which bed sheets are made
Shirting	/ any various fabrics used to make men's shirts
Silesia	/ sturdy twill-weave cotton fabric; used for pockets and linings
Silk	/ fabric made from the fine threads produced by certain insect larvae
Spandex	/ elastic synthetic fabric
Sponge Cloth	/ any soft porous fabric (especially in a loose honeycomb weave)
Stammel	/ coarse woolen cloth formerly used for undergarments and usually dyed bright red
Suede	/ fabric made to resemble suede leather
Suiting	/ fabric used for suits
Swan's Down	/ soft woolen fabric used especially for baby clothes
Taffeta	/ crisp smooth lustrous fabric
Tammy	/ plain-woven (often glazed) fabric of wool or wool and cotton used especially formerly for linings and garments and curtains
Tapa	/ paper-like cloth made in the South Pacific by pounding tapa bark
Tapestry	/ heavy textile with woven design; used for curtains, upholstery
Tartan	/ cloth having a crisscross design
Terry	/ pile fabric (usually cotton) with uncut loops on both sides; used to make bath towels and bath robes
Ticking	/ strong fabric used for mattresses and pillow covers
Toweling	/ any fabrics (linen or cotton) used to make towels
Tweed	/ thick woolen fabric used for clothing; originated in Scotland
Twill	/ cloth with parallel diagonal lines or ribs
Velcro	/ (trademark) nylon fabric used as a fastening
Velours	/ heavy fabric that resembles velvet
Velvet	/ silky densely piled fabric with a plain back
Velveteen	/ usually cotton fabric with a short pile imitating velvet
Vicuna	/ soft woolen fabric made from the fleece of the vicuna
Viyella	/ (trademark) a fabric made from a twilled mixture of cotton and wool
Voile	/ light semi-transparent plain-weave fabric
Waterproof	/ any fabric impervious to water
Webbing	/ strong fabric woven in strips
Whipcord	/ strong worsted or cotton fabric with a diagonal rib
Wincey	/ (British) a plain or twilled fabric of wool and cotton used especially for warm shirts or skirts and pajamas
Wire Cloth	/ fabric woven of metallic wire
Wool	/ fabric made from the hair of sheep
Worsted	/ woolen fabric with a hard textured surface and no nap; woven of worsted yarns

THEY SAID
PRÊT-À-PORTER
WILL KILL YOUR
NAME, AND IT
SAVED ME.

/ PIERRE CARDIN

06 MANUFACTURING

PRODUCT DEVELOPMENT / DESIGN
STUDIO AND FACTORY / FLAT PATTERN /
SEWING DETAIL / EMBELLISHMENT /
LABEL / PACKAGING / FABRIC SOURCING

6.1 PRODUCT DEVELOPMENT

AND WHERE YOU SHOULD REFER TO IN THIS BOO

PLANNING   DEVELOPMENT

1 EVALUATE MERCHANDISE MIX

P.30
- Classify of product type by: color, style, product type, material, etc.
- Classify products into groups, categories, subcategories, etc.

2 MERCHANDISE FORECAST

- Sales history
- Selling periods
P.30
- Product types
- Price points
P.318
- Size ranges

3 MERCHANDISE BUDGET PLANNING

- Costs & price ranges
- Discounts
- Markups

4 MERCHANDISE ASSORTMENT PLANNING

- Basic stock
- Replenishment

5 UPDATE MERCHANDISE PLANNING DURING LINE DEVELOPMENT

- Update budgets
- Update assortments
- Develop delivery plans

1 CONCEPT DEVELOPMENT

P.10
- Integrate current trends
  - / economic
  - / social
  - / cultural
  - / technological
  - / demographic
  - / lifestyle
  - / target market evaluation
- Describe fashion trends
  - / color
  - / line & silhouette   P.28
P.146
  - / detail
  - / pattern & print
  - / fit
  - / style   P.17
- Establish line direction
  - / color palette
  - / styling guidelines
P.165
    (including accessories)
  - / styles   P.17
P.204
- Describe materials
  - / fiber content
  - / yarn type
  - / fabric structure
  - / finishing
- Identify group concepts
  - / separates
  - / related separates
  - / coordinates
- Analyze current line
  - / continued styles
  - / modified styles
  - / new designs
  - / fashionable & basic items

265

MANUFACTURING

Product Development / Design Studio & Factory / Flat Pattern / Sewing Detail / Embellishment / Label / Packaging / Fabric Sourcing

PRESENTATION

2 PRODUCT DEVELOPMENT

- Develop designs

P.30
  - / design sketches
  - / first patterns
  - / design specifications
  - / fit standards   P.318
P.204
  - / material descriptions
  - / embellishments   P.284

- Create design prototypes

  - / review prototypes
  - / style testing
  - / fitting evaluation
  - / fabric evaluation
  - / evaluate assembly methods

- Revise pattern prototypes until perfection

3 LINE ADOPTION

- Assign styles / sizes / colors / materials to line plan

- Balance product assortments

  - / variety
  - / volume
  - / diversity
  - / allocation

- Produce samples for fashion show / photo shoot / catalog

4 TECHNICAL DESIGN DEVELOPMENT

- Perfect styling and fit

- Engineer production patterns & grading

- Develop & test styles / quality specifications

  - / styling
  - / fit
  - / materials
  - / assembly methods

1 INTERNAL

- Review for adoption

  - / line concept
  - / image strategy
  - / catagories
  - / design specs & costing
  - / pricing strategy

2 WHOLESALE

- Line preview

  - / line concept
  - / image strategy
  - / assortment strategy
  - / style appeal
  - / marketing strategy
  - / pricing strategy
  - / visual merchandising

- Line / Style release

  - / fashion shows
  - / wholesale markets
  - / sales presentations
  - / trunk shows

3 RETAIL

- Marketing

  - / press release
  - / catalog
  - / television
  - / magazine / multi-media
  - / social media / blog / facebook / instagram, etc.

- Visual merchandising

  - / lighting
  - / signage
  - / floor plan
  - / window and props display

- Labels & packaging

- Customer service

6.2 DESIGN STUDIO AND FACTORY

WHAT'S INSIDE A DESIGN STUDIO?

Mood /
Inspiration Board

Computer

Half-size
Dress Fo

Scanner &
Printer

Fashion
Magazine

Sketch
Book

Graphic /
Pen Tablet

267

MANUFACTURING

Product Development / **Design Studio & Factory** / Flat Pattern / Sewing Detail / Embellishment / Label / Packaging / Fabric Sourcing

Theme Board

Fabric
Swatch

Fashion
Reference Books

Clothes
Rack

Trend Reports

THEME

Fabric
Swatches

Fabric
Swatches

Garment
Samples

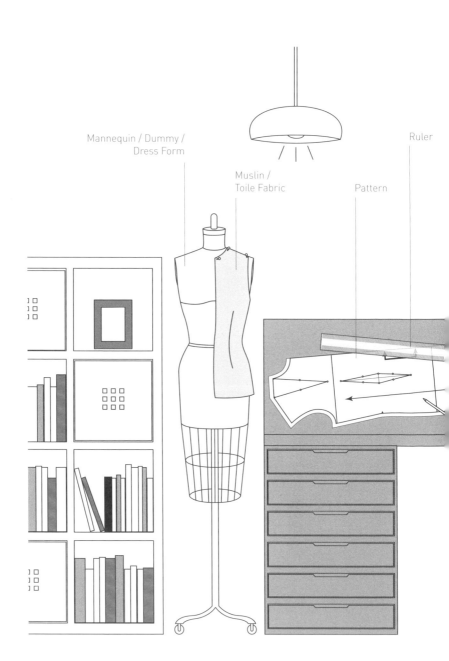

Mannequin / Dummy /
Dress Form

Muslin /
Toile Fabric

Pattern

Ruler

269

MANUFACTURING

Product Development / **Design Studio & Factory** / Flat Pattern / Sewing Detail / Embellishment / Label / Packaging / Fabric Sourcing

Full-body
Mannequin / Dummy /
Dress Form

Pattern
Paper

Ironing
Board

Iron

Cabinet

French
Curve

Muslin /
Toile Fabric

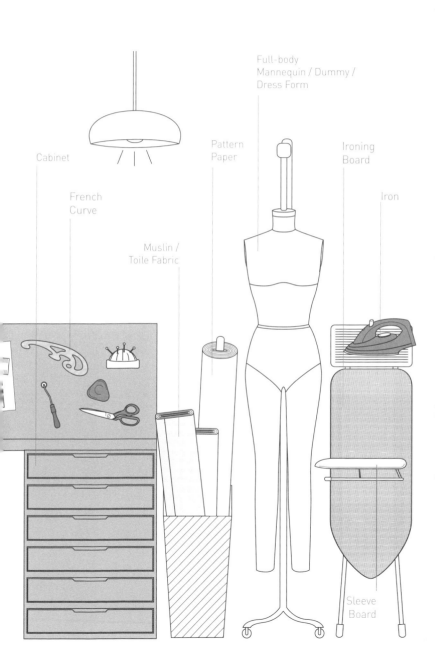

Sleeve
Board

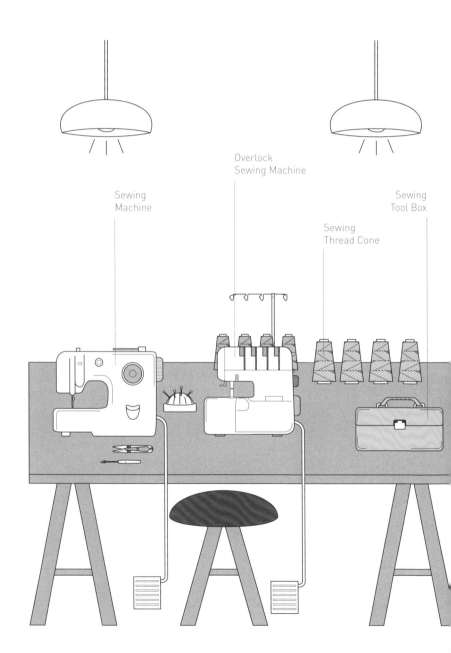

Overlock
Sewing Machine

Sewing
Machine

Sewing
Tool Box

Sewing
Thread Cone

271

MANUFACTURING

Product Development / **Design Studio & Factory** / Flat Pattern / Sewing Detail / Embellishment / Label / Packaging / Fabric Sourcing

SEWING TOOL BOX
WHAT'S INSIDE?

Tailor's Chalk

Bobbin

Bobbin Case

Pin Cushion

Needle

Pinking Shears

Safety Pin

Pin

Tweezer

Tracing Wheel

Awl

Thimble

Needle Threader

Dressmaking Scissors

Seam Ripper

Loop Turner

Point Turner

Thread Snips

Tape Measure

WHAT'S INSIDE A GARMENT FACTORY?

Industrial
Sewing Machine

Computerized
Cutting System

Straight
Knife Cutter

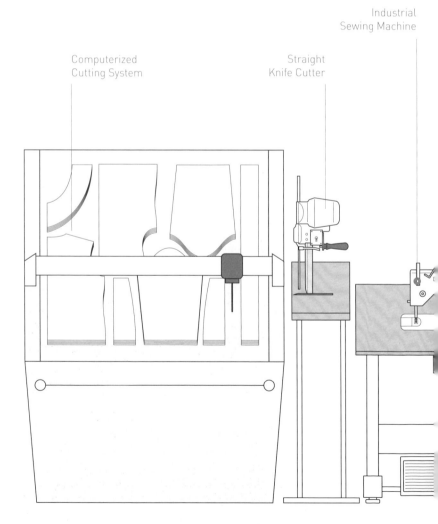

273

MANUFACTURING

Product Development / **Design Studio & Factory** / Flat Pattern / Sewing Detail / Embellishment / Label / Packaging / Fabric Sourcing

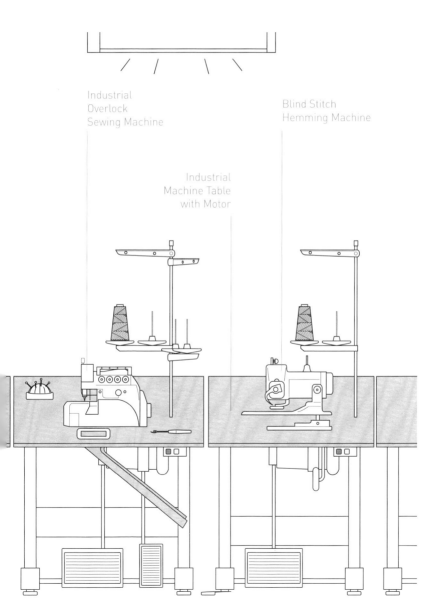

Industrial
Overlock
Sewing Machine

Blind Stitch
Hemming Machine

Industrial
Machine Table
with Motor

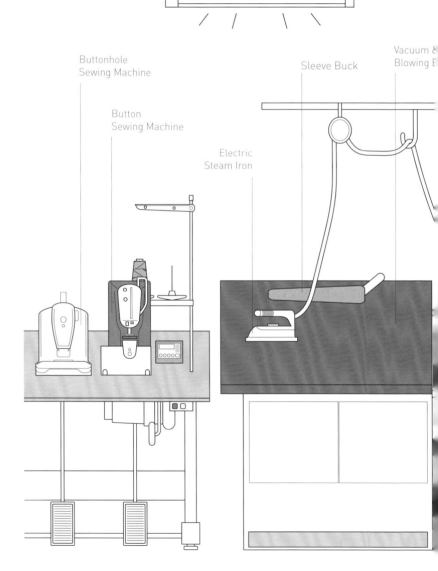

Buttonhole
Sewing Machine

Button
Sewing Machine

Electric
Steam Iron

Sleeve Buck

Vacuum &
Blowing B

275

MANUFACTURING

Product Development / **Design Studio & Factory** / Flat Pattern / Sewing Detail / Embellishment / Label / Packaging / Fabric Sourcing

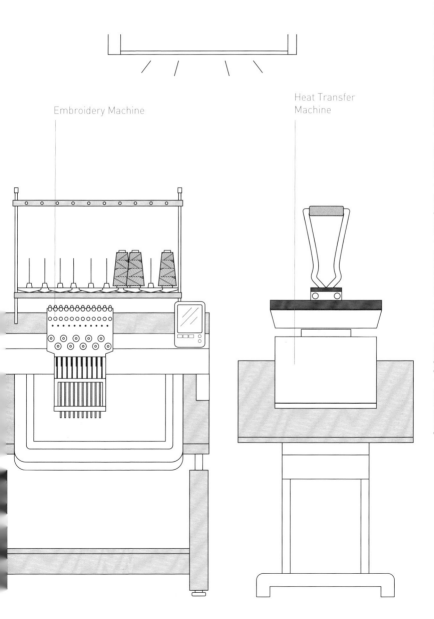

Embroidery Machine

Heat Transfer
Machine

6.3 FLAT PATTERN

PATTERN MARKINGS

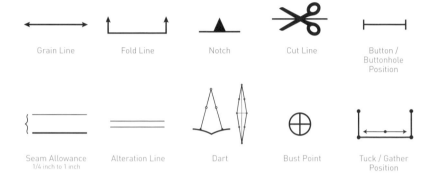

| Grain Line | Fold Line | Notch | Cut Line | Button / Buttonhole Position |

| Seam Allowance 1/4 inch to 1 inch | Alteration Line | Dart | Bust Point | Tuck / Gather Position |

PATTERN MARKINGS ON FRONT BODICE

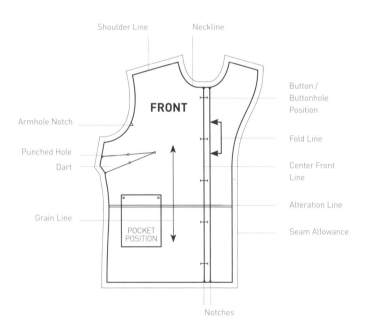

Shoulder Line

Neckline

FRONT

Button / Buttonhole Position

Armhole Notch

Fold Line

Punched Hole

Dart

Center Front Line

Alteration Line

Grain Line

POCKET POSITION

Seam Allowance

Notches

MANUFACTURING

Product Development / Design Studio & Factory / **Flat Pattern** / Sewing Detail / Embellishment / Label / Packaging / Fabric Sourcing

PATTERN MARKINGS ON BACK BODICE

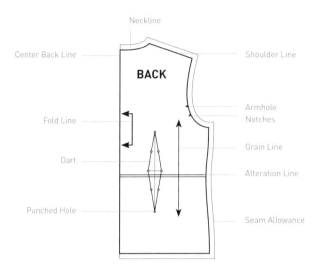

Neckline

Center Back Line

BACK

Shoulder Line

Fold Line

Armhole Notches

Dart

Grain Line

Alteration Line

Punched Hole

Seam Allowance

PATTERN MARKINGS ON SLEEVES

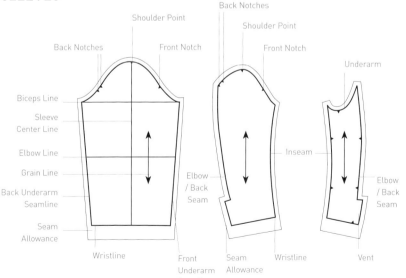

Shoulder Point

Back Notches

Back Notches

Shoulder Point

Front Notch

Front Notch

Underarm

Biceps Line

Sleeve Center Line

Elbow Line

Grain Line

Inseam

Elbow / Back Seam

Elbow / Back Seam

Back Underarm Seamline

Seam Allowance

Seam Allowance

Wristline

Wristline

Front Underarm Seamline

Seam Allowance

Vent

ONE-PIECE SLEEVE

TWO-PIECE SLEEVE

PATTERN MARKINGS ON DRESSES

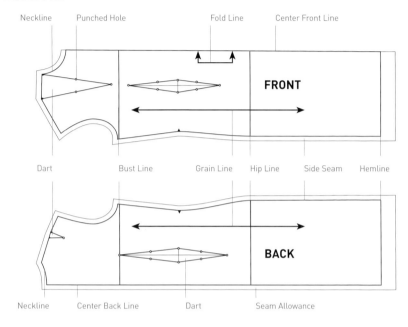

Neckline · Punched Hole · Fold Line · Center Front Line

FRONT

Dart · Bust Line · Grain Line · Hip Line · Side Seam · Hemline

BACK

Neckline · Center Back Line · Dart · Seam Allowance

PATTERN MARKINGS ON PANTS

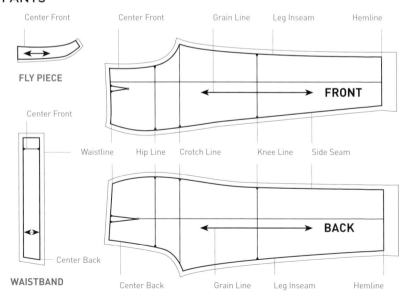

Center Front · Center Front · Grain Line · Leg Inseam · Hemline

FLY PIECE

FRONT

Center Front

Waistline · Hip Line · Crotch Line · Knee Line · Side Seam

BACK

Center Back

WAISTBAND

Center Back · Grain Line · Leg Inseam · Hemline

DUMMY ANATOMY

MANUFACTURING

Product Development / Design Studio & Factory / **Flat Pattern** / Sewing Detail / Embellishment / Label / Packaging / Fabric Sourcing

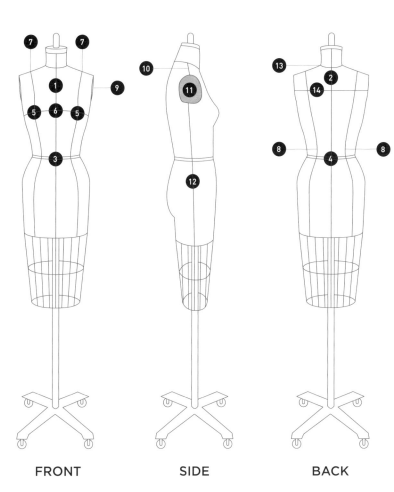

FRONT   **SIDE**   **BACK**

1 Center Front (CF)	6 Center Front Bust Level	11 Armhole Plate
2 Center Back (CB)	7 Side Front	12 Side Seam (SS)
3 Front Waist	8 Side Back	13 High Point Shoulder
4 Back Waist	9 Mid-armhole	14 Horizontal Balance Line
5 Bust Points	10 Shoulder Line	

6.4 SEWING DETAIL

DARTS

Vertical Dart

Bust Dart

Center Dart

Armhole Dart

French Dart

Neckline Dart

DART STRUCTURE

Shoulder Dart

Fisheye Dart

Double Dart

Waistline Dart

Closed Dart

Open Dart

PLEATS

Accordion / Knife Pleat

Box Pleat

Inverted Box Pleat

Side Pleat

Double Box Pleat

Cartridge Pleat

Kick Pleat

Fortuny Pleat

Fluted Pleat

Honeycomb Pleat

Rolled Pleat

Sunburst Pleat

TUCKS

Tuck

Pin Tuck

Piped Tuck

GATHERING

Gathering

Shirring

Smocking

281

MANUFACTURING

Product Development / Design Studio & Factory / Flat Pattern / **Sewing Detail** / Embellishment / Label / Packaging / Fabric Sourcing

STITCH CLASSES

100 - Class Stitches

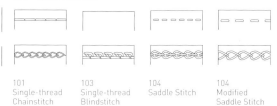

101
Single-thread
Chainstitch

103
Single-thread
Blindstitch

104
Saddle Stitch

104
Modified
Saddle Stitch

200 - Class Stitches

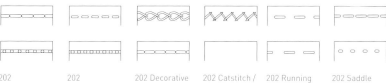

202
Backstitch

202
Prickstitch

202 Decorative
Chainstitch

202 Catstitch /
Herringbone
Stitch

202 Running
Stitch

202 Saddle
Stitch

300 - Class Stitches

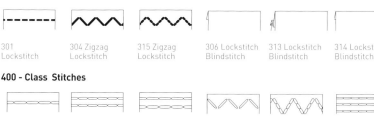

301
Lockstitch

304 Zigzag
Lockstitch

315 Zigzag
Lockstitch

306 Lockstitch
Blindstitch

313 Lockstitch
Blindstitch

314 Lockstitch
Blindstitch

400 - Class Stitches

401
Two-thread
Chainstitch

402 Cording
Stitch

406 Cover
Seaming Stitch

404 Zigzag
Chainstitch

404 Multi-
step Zigzag
Chainstitch

407 Cover
Seaming Stitch
attaching elastic

500 - Class Stitches

501 (1-thread)

502 (2-thread)

503 (3-thread)

504 (3-thread)

505 (3-thread)

512 (3-thread)

600 - Class Stitches

FRONT

BACK

514 (4-thread)

515 (4-thread)

602 Cover
Stitch

605 Cover
Stitch

607 Flat
Seaming Stitch

SEAM CLASSES

Superimposed Seams

Seam Drawing							
Seam Code	SSa (1.01.01)	SSe (1.06.03)	SSq (2.42.04)	SSh (4.04.01)	SSat (5.06.01)	SSw (2.04.06)	SSag (4.10.02)
Name	Plain Seam	French Seam	Yoking	Cover Seam	Setting Stripe	Mock Felled Seam	Seaming
Common Application	General seaming	Edges of collars	Attach yokes	Sweatshirt seams	Attach stripes	Side seams of shirts	Tap the neck-line of T-shirts

Lapped Seams

Seam Drawing							
Seam Code	LSa (2.01.01)	LSb (2.02.01)	LSd (5.31.01)	LSc (2.04.06)	LSe (1.22.01)	LSq (2.02.03)	LSr (2.06.02)
Name	Lap Seaming	/	Patch Pocket Setting	Felled Seam	Yoking	Welt Seam	Sleeve Set
Common Application	Attach knit cuffs	Side seam of jeans, less common than LSq	Patch pockets	Side seam of jeans	Yokes (less common than SSq)	Side seams of shirts	Setting sleeves

Edge Seams

Seam Drawing							
Seam Code	EFa (6.02.01)	EFb (6.03.01)	EFc(6.06.01)	EFd (6.01.01)	EFh	EFp (8.06.01)	EFr (7.26.05)
Name	/	Clean Finish Hem	Blind Hemming	Serging	Belt Loops	/	Tunnelled Elastic
Common Application	Hem on knits	Shirttail hems	T-shirt hems	Serging pants panels, fly, etc.	Belt loops	Making straps	Insert elastic bands

Bound Seams

Seam Drawing							
Seam Code	BSa(3.01.01)	BSb(3.03.01)	BSc(3.05.01)	BSg (3.14.01)	BSj(3.05.06)	BSe (3.14.01)	BSf mod
Name	/	/	/	Binding	/	/	/
Common Application	Foldover braids	Binding edges	Piping	Clean finish binding	Clean finish binding	Seaming & binding on outerwear	Topstitch hidden in seam line

Flat Seams

FSa (4.01.01)	FSb (4.02.01)	FSc (4.03.02)	FSf
Flatseaming	/	/	/
Underwear flatseaming	/	/	Bolt end seaming

Ornamental Seams

OSa (5.01.01)	OSd (5.20.01)	OSf (6.05.01)
Decorative Sitch	Tunnel	/
Jeans back pockets	Tunnelled gathering waist	Sewing darts

HEM & OTHER EDGE FINISHINGS

MANUFACTURING

Product Development / Design Studio & Factory / Flat Pattern / **Sewing Detail** / Embellishment / Label / Packaging / Fabric Sourcing

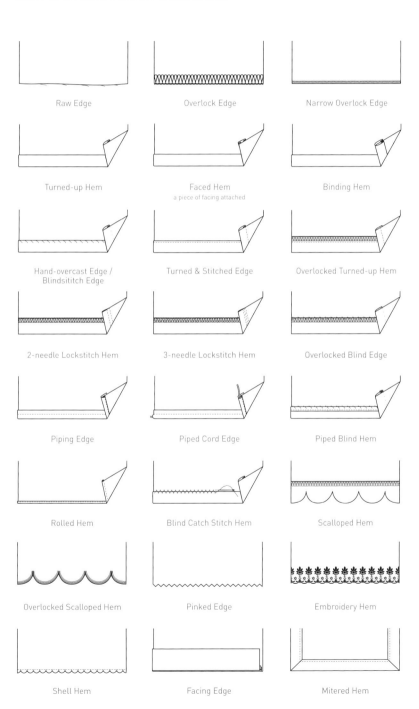

Raw Edge

Overlock Edge

Narrow Overlock Edge

Turned-up Hem

Faced Hem
a piece of facing attached

Binding Hem

Hand-overcast Edge /
Blindsititch Edge

Turned & Stitched Edge

Overlocked Turned-up Hem

2-needle Lockstitch Hem

3-needle Lockstitch Hem

Overlocked Blind Edge

Piping Edge

Piped Cord Edge

Piped Blind Hem

Rolled Hem

Blind Catch Stitch Hem

Scalloped Hem

Overlocked Scalloped Hem

Pinked Edge

Embroidery Hem

Shell Hem

Facing Edge

Mitered Hem

6.5 EMBELLISHMENT

BUTTONS

2-hole Flat

4-hole Flat

Flat Shank

Quarter Shank

Half Shank

Full Shank

Covered

Toggle

Knot

Beaded

Mandarin /
Frog

Faceted

Carved

Heart-
shaped

Crest

Jeans

SNAP / PRESS BUTTONS

Button

Stud

Socket

Eyelet

Baby Durable Dot Snap Fastener

Press Button

BUTTON STITCHING

Two holes
with
horizontal
stitching

Four holes
with
parallel
stitching

Parallel
stitching &
crossover

Parallel
stitching &
S-crossover

Parallel
stitching &
Z-crossover

X-stitching

X-stitching &
crossover

BUTTONHOLES

Machine
Keyhole

Fishtail
Keyhole

Machine
Square

Machine
Round

Radial
Straight

Eyelet
Taper

Bound

285

MANUFACTURING

Product Development / Design Studio & Factory / Flat Pattern / Sewing Detail / **Embellishment** / Label / Packaging / Fabric Sourcing

BUCKLES & SLIDERS

Buckle Set

Fashion Buckle

Half Roller Buckle

Double Tongue Roller Buckle

Full Skate Buckle

Half Solid Brass Buckle

Full Shoe Buckle

Full Buckle

Interlocking Buckle

Bolt Snap / Trigger Hook

Cam Buckle

Concealed Hook Buckle

Brass Slide

Full Slider

PLASTIC BUCKLES & SLIDERS

Side Release

Tri-Glide

Strap Adjuster

Keeper & Step Lock

Center Release

Split Release

Reducing Loop

Tri-Loop

Plastic D-Ring

Plastic Rectangle Ring

Rotate Snap Hook

Cord Lock

HOOK & EYE FASTENERS

Hook & Eye Buckle

Over-latch Clasp

Hook & Bar

Slide Hook

Hook & Eye

Covered Hook & Eye

RINGS

Flat Ring

Light Ring

Heavy Ring

Solid Brass Ring

Split Ring

RECTANGLE RINGS

Wire Square Ring

Wide Wire Rectangle Ring

D-RINGS

Heavy D-Ring

Light D-Ring

Unwelded D-Ring

Welded D-Ring

CORNERS

Collar Tip

Engraved Collar Tip

RIVETS

ROCKET SPIKES

Bifurcated
Rivet

Pyramid
Rivet

Double
Capped Rivet

Tubular /
Self Piercing
Rivet

Pyramid
Spike

Cone Spike

EYELETS & WASHERS

Small Eyelet
& Washer

Large Eyelet
& Washer

Oval Eyelet &
Washer

Floral-shaped
Eyelet &
Washer

D Ring
Shoelace Eye

SEQUINS

Cup Sequin

Flat Sequin

Flat Paillette

Star Sequin

Heart Sequin

Leaf Sequin

BEADS

Seed Bead

Bugle Bead

Metal Bead

Wood Bead

Navette
Gemstone

Rectangular
Gemstone

Faceted Oval
Bead

Faceted
Round Bead

Pear Faceted
Gemstone
with Mount

Baguette
Faceted
Gemstone
with Mount

Navette
Faceted
Gemstone
with Mount

Rhinestone Motif

Beaded Motif

287

MANUFACTURING

Product Development / Design Studio & Factory / Flat Pattern / Sewing Detail / Embellishment / Label / Packaging / Fabric Sourcing

ZIPPERS

Closed End

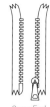

Open End

Invisible

Two-way /
Bottom-to-
bottom

Bag Type/
Head-to-
head

ZIPPER TEETH

Molded Plastic Teeth

Coil Nylon Teeth

Metal Teeth

ZIPPER SLIDERS

Non-lock
Slider

Auto-lock
Slider

Pin lock
Slider

Double
Pull

Key Lock
Slider

Cord
Pull

Chain
Pull

Tape
Pull

Leather
Pull

Silicon
Pull

TRIMMING

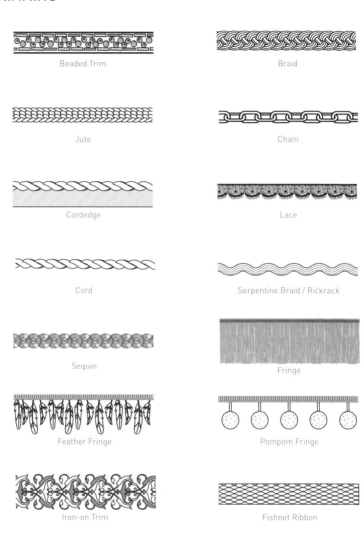

Beaded Trim

Braid

Jute

Chain

Cordedge

Lace

Cord

Serpentine Braid / Rickrack

Sequin

Fringe

Feather Fringe

Pompom Fringe

Iron-on Trim

Fishnet Ribbon

Leather Tape

Rhinestone

Snap Tape

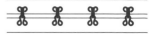

Hook & Eye Tape

289

MANUFACTURING

Product Development / Design Studio & Factory / Flat Pattern / Sewing Detail / **Embellishment** / Label / Packaging / Fabric Sourcing

CHAIN

Curb Chain

Double Curb Chain

Figaro Chain

Trace Chain
uniform breadth and thickness,
delicate and in finer width

Rolo / Belcher Chain

Cable Chain

Double Link Cable Chain

Double Cable Chain

Garibaldi Chain

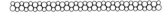

Byzantine Chain

Popcorn Chain

Ball Chain

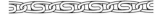

Cobra Chain

Scroll Chain

Venetian / Box Chain

Anchor Chain

Bar Chain

Barley Corn Chain

Foxtail Chain

Spiga Chain

Snake Chain

Cocoon Chain

Omega Chain

French Rope Chain

Panther Chain

Herringbone Chain

6.6 LABEL

COMMON GARMENT LABELS AND DESCRIPTION

Main Label	/ shows the brand name or logo of a company
Size Label	/ defines a specific set of measurements of the human body
Flag Label	/ sewn at outside of the side seam. Flag labels normally include a brand logo or name and are used as a design feature
Care Label	/ shows the washing and ironing instruction
Manufacturer Label	/ shows the manufacturer's code given by buyers. Most of the international buyers source garments from different parts of the world. In case buyers need to track the manufacturer of a particular product, they use this code
Other Special Labels	/ show other information customers or buyers want to know. For example, batch mark, country of origin, fiber content of the garment, etc.

COMMON LABEL PLACEMENT POSITIONS

MANUFACTURING

Product Development / Design Studio & Factory / Flat Pattern / Sewing Detail / Embellishment / **Label** / Packaging / Fabric Sourcing

HANGTAG DESIGN EXAMPLES

6.7 **PACKAGING**

CARTON BOX TYPES

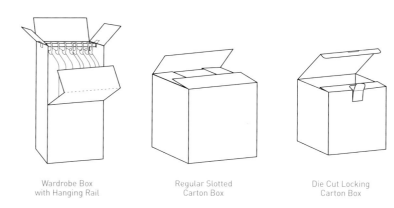

Wardrobe Box
with Hanging Rail

Regular Slotted
Carton Box

Die Cut Locking
Carton Box

GIFT BOX TYPES

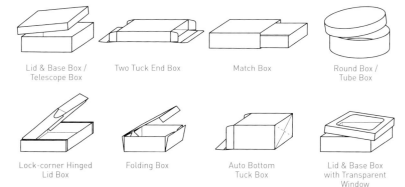

Lid & Base Box /
Telescope Box

Two Tuck End Box

Match Box

Round Box /
Tube Box

Lock-corner Hinged
Lid Box

Folding Box

Auto Bottom
Tuck Box

Lid & Base Box
with Transparent
Window

OTHER PACKAGING

Transparent Polybag

Wrapping Tissue Paper

Dust Bag

6.8 **FABRIC SOURCING**

Asia	China	Beijing	**1**	Muxiyuan Fabric Market
		Shanghai	**2**	South Bund Fabric Market
		Guangzhou	**3**	Zhongda Fabric Market
		Hangzhou	**4**	Sijiqing Fabric Market
		Shenzhen	**5**	Dongmen Fabric Market
		Hong Kong	**6**	Sham Shui Po
	Japan	Tokyo	**7**	Nippori Textile Town
	Thailand	Bangkok	**8**	Phahurat Market
	South Korea	Seoul	**9**	Dongdaemun Fabric Market
		Seoul	**10**	Gwangjang Market
	Vietnam	Hanoi	**11**	Ninh Hiep Fabric Market
	India	Mumbai	**12**	Mangaldas Market
		New Delhi	**13**	Gandhi Nagar Textile Market
		Gujarat	**14**	Surat Textile Market

295

MANUFACTURING

Product Development / Design Studio & Factory / Flat Pattern / Sewing Detail / Embellishment / Label / Packaging / Fabric Sourcing

Asia	Taiwan	Taipei	**15**	Yongle Fabric Market
	Singapore	Singapore	**16**	Textile Centre
Europe	France	Paris	**17**	Marché Saint Pierre
	United Kingdom	London	**18**	Goldhawk Road
	Italy	Rome	**19**	Fratelli Bassetti Tessuti
	Turkey	Istanbul	**20**	Mahmutpasha Bazaar
America	USA	New York City	**21**	Midtown Manhattan - Garment District
		Los Angeles	**22**	LA Fashion District
	Mexico	Mexico City	**23**	Centro Historico
	Brazil	São Paulo	**24**	Rua 25 de Março

I LIKE THE BODY.
I LIKE TO DESIGN
EVERYTHING TO
DO WITH THE
BODY.

/ GIANNI VERSACE

07 BODY & BEAUTY

BODY / HAIR / COSMETICS / PERFUME

7.1 BODY

WOMEN'S BODY TERMINOLOGY

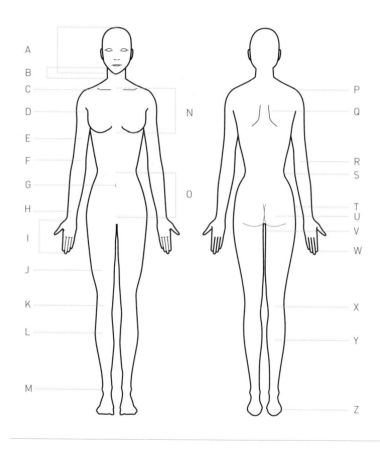

A	Head	H	Wrist
B	Neck	I	Hand
C	Collarbone	J	Thigh
D	Armpit	K	Knee
E	Upper Arm	L	Leg
F	Front of Elbow	M	Ankle
G	Navel	N	Breast (for women) / Chest (for men)

MEN'S BODY TERMINOLOGY

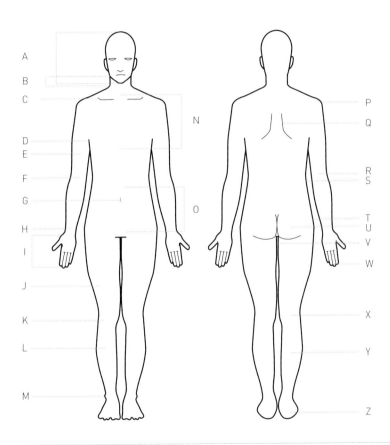

O   Abdomen
P   Shoulder
Q   Shoulder Blade
R   Elbow
S   Waist
T   Hip
U   Buttock

V   Crotch
W   Finger
X   Back of Knee
Y   Calf
Z   Foot

WOMEN'S BODY SHAPES

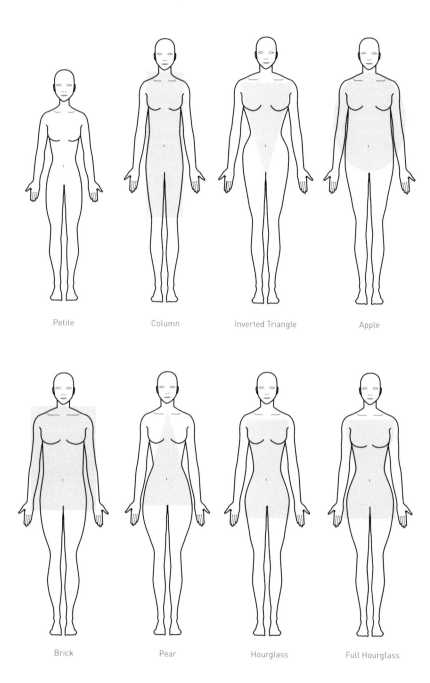

Petite

Column

Inverted Triangle

Apple

Brick

Pear

Hourglass

Full Hourglass

MEN'S BODY SHAPES

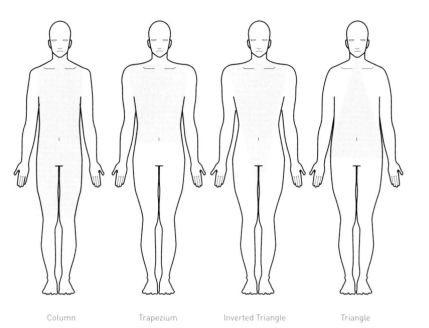

Column   Trapezium   Inverted Triangle   Triangle

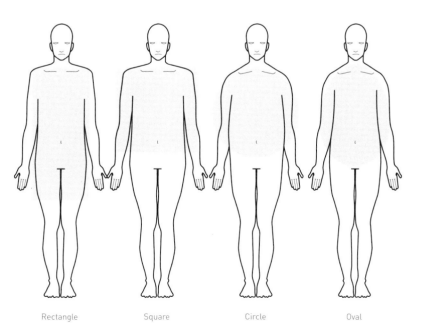

Rectangle   Square   Circle   Oval

TERMINOLOGY FOR THE HEAD

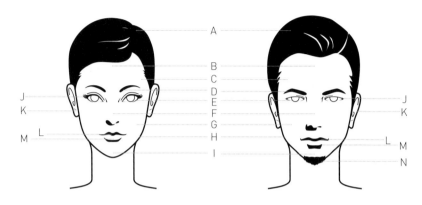

A	Hair		H	Jaw
B	Forehead		I	Chin
C	Temple		J	Eyelash
D	Eyebrow		K	Ear
E	Eye		L	Mouth
F	Nose		M	Lip
G	Cheek		N	Beard

FACE SHAPES

Oval

Oblong

Square

Inverted Triangle

Diamond

Round

Heart-shaped

Rectangle

TERMINOLOGY FOR THE HAND

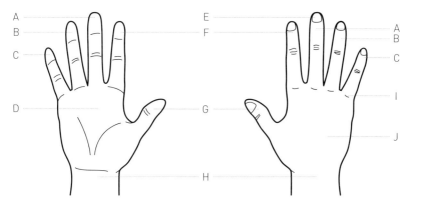

A	Middle Finger	F	Index Finger
B	Ring Finger	G	Thumb
C	Little Finger / Pinky Finger	H	Wrist
D	Palm	I	Knuckle
E	Fingernail / Nail	J	Back of the Hand

TERMINOLOGY FOR THE FOOT

A   Forefoot
B   Midfoot
C   Hindfoot
D   Hallux / Big Toe
E   2nd, 3rd, 4th & Little Toes
F   1st Metatarsal Head
G   2nd & 3rd Metatarsal Heads
H   4th & 5th Metatarsal Heads
I   Arch
J   Lateral Midfoot
K   Inner Heel
L   Heel Front
M   Heel
N   Outer Heel
O   Ankle
P   Rearfoot
Q   Toenail
R   Upper Part of the Foot
S   Sole
T   Achilles Tendon

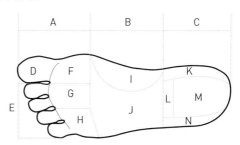

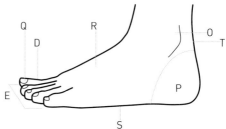

7.2 # HAIR

COMMON WOMEN'S HAIRSTYLES

Bob

Box Bob /
Short Bob

Short Bob /
Graduated Bob

Curl Under /
Page Boy

Bowl Cu

Asymmetric
Cut

Pixie Cut

Shag

Kiss Curls

Finger Wa
Marcelli

Curly Hair

Wavy Hair

One Length

Layered Cut

Hime C

Afro

Spiral Afro Curls /
Ringlets

Feathered
Hair

Blowout

Braid /
Plait

Bunches /
Pigtail

All Back /
Brushed Back

Ponytail

Bun

French Twist

Beehive

Bouffant

Cornrows

COMMON MEN'S HAIRSTYLES

Side Part

Crew Cut

Caesar Cut

Quiff

Wings

Curtained Hair

Spiky Hair

Fauxhawk

Emo

Devilock

Afro

Dreadlocks / Dreads

High and Tight

Man Bun

Top Knot

Shape-Up

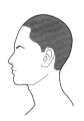

Skinhead

Fade

Undercut

Pompadour

Hi-top Fade

Mullet

Dreadhawk

Mohawk Cut /
Mohican

HAIR COMB TYPES

Bristle Paddle Brush	Nylon Paddle Brush	Parting Comb / Rat Tail Comb	Bristle Round Brush	Detangler Brush
/ Natural bristles stimulate the scalp for better blood circulation / Best for medium to long hair / Useful for untangling hair	/ With rounded pins / Massages the scalp and distributes natural hair oils / For fine hair or brushing wet hair	/ For parting hair into sections / Smooths hair	/ Natural bristles stimulate the scalp for better blood circulation / Distributes natural oils for shinier, more manageable hair / For smooth blowouts	/ A mix of bristles in varying lengths / Best at removing knots and tangles

HAIR ACCESSORIES

Alice Band

Headband

Bra Strap Headband

Comb Alice Band

Tiara

Hair Comb

Hair Bow

Chignon Cover

Hairnet

Hair Slide / Bobby Pin

Hair Slide

Hair Stick

Hair Claw

Barrette

Snap Barrette

Scrunchie

Pony Cuff

Ponytail Holder / Hair Tie

7.3 **COSMETICS**

MAKEUP STEP-BY-STEP

MOISTURIZER

/ Wash the face
/ Apply moisturizer
/ It smooths and keeps the skin supple

PRIMER

/ Apply primer on the face and neck
/ It minimizes pores and conceals any flaws on the skin

CONCEALER

/ Dab carefully over the problem area and blend with fingertips
/ It covers any blemishes on the skin

FOUNDATION

/ Apply small patches to the chin, cheeks and forehead
/ Blend to cover the entire face

HIGHLIGHTER & BRONZER

/ Apply to the area desired and blend
/ It makes the face look more defined

BLUSH

/ Apply to the apples of the cheeks
/ It gives the face a pleasant glow

EYEBROW PENCIL

/ Draw along the natural line of the eyebrow
/ Color in slightly lighter than the hair

EYESHADOW, LINER & MASCARA

/ Use three shades of eyeshadow, starting with the lightest color
/ Apply eyeliner and mascara

LIPSTICK, LINER & GLOSS

/ Finish the look by applying lip makeup
/ May apply a layer of lip gloss

HIGHLIGHTING AND CONTOURING

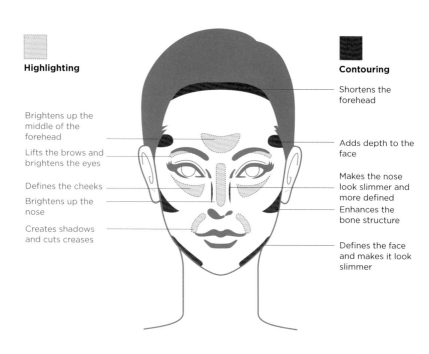

Highlighting

Brightens up the middle of the forehead

Lifts the brows and brightens the eyes

Defines the cheeks

Brightens up the nose

Creates shadows and cuts creases

Contouring

Shortens the forehead

Adds depth to the face

Makes the nose look slimmer and more defined

Enhances the bone structure

Defines the face and makes it look slimmer

HIGHLIGHTING & CONTOURING FOR DIFFERENT FACE SHAPES

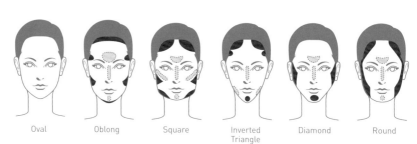

Oval   Oblong   Square   Inverted Triangle   Diamond   Round

MAKEUP PRODUCTS

FOR FACE

Primer

Liquid
Foundation

Powder
Foundation

Spray
Foundation

Setting Powder /
Loose Powder

Concealer

Bronzer

Luminizer

Blush

Shimmer
& Glitter

FOR EYES

Eye Primer

Eyeshadow

Eyeliner

Mascara

False Lashes

FOR EYEBROWS

Eyebrow Pencil

Eyebrow Powder

FOR LIPS

Lip Primer

Lip Pencil

Lipstick

Lip Gloss

MAKEUP TOOLS

BRUSHES

Fan Brush

/ For applying highlighter and blush
/ Creates gentle contours

Flat Foundation Brush

/ For applying liquid foundation
/ For applying and blending concealer

Foundation Brush

/ For applying liquid foundation and concealer
/ For blending cream products

Flat Top Brush

/ For applying and blending liquid or cream foundation
/ For applying powder for full coverage

Angled Foundation Brush

/ For applying liquid or cream foundation
/ For blending concealer
/ For blending cream blush and bronzer

Powder Brush

/ For applying powder foundation, powder blush, bronzer and highlighter
/ For applying products to the body

Round Buffing Brush

/ For applying and blending foundation and concealer
/ Controls color
/ Contours

Stippling Brush

/ For applying liquid or cream foundation
/ For applying highlighter and blush

Angled Blush Brush

/ For applying blush, bronzer and highlighter
/ Contours cheekbones and other features

Blush Brush

/ Its small size allows precise application
/ For applying and blending blush, bronzer and highlighter

OTHER MAKEUP TOOLS

Lash Curler

Tweezer

Sharpeners

Air Brush

Sponge / Applicator

Eyebrow Brush & Lash Comb

Safety Scissors

Nail Files

Blotting Paper

Mirror

EYELINE & EYEBROW STYLES

EYELINE STYLES

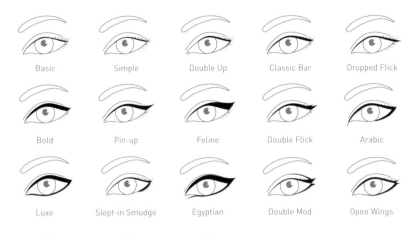

Basic	Simple	Double Up	Classic Bar	Dropped Flick
Bold	Pin-up	Feline	Double Flick	Arabic
Luxe	Slept-in Smudge	Egyptian	Double Mod	Open Wings
Drama	Soft Smoke	Panda Smudge		

EYEBROW SHAPING

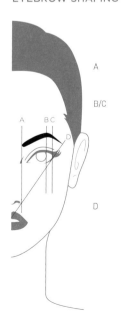

A — Line up the inner edge of the brow with the outside of the corresponding nostril (A).

B/C — The highest point of the arch should be just at the outer edge of the iris (B). However, a more sophisticated eye is achieved when the highest point occurs at the outer corner of the eyeball (C), depending on the face shape. Anywhere between B & C is optimal.

D — The outer brow should taper off to a point that intersects with an imaginary line drawn from the center of lips, past the outer nostril, to the outer edge of the eye (D).

EYEBROW STYLES

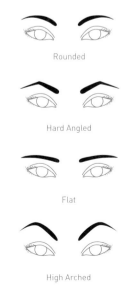

Rounded

Hard Angled

Flat

High Arched

LIPS

LIP MAKEUP STEP-BY-STEP

| Create an 'x' on the upper lip and an outline in the middle of the lower lip | Fill the two parts | Outline the upper lip | Fill the upper lip | Fill the lower lip |

LIP SHAPES

| Thin Lower | Oval | Thin Upper | Downturned | Thin | Large Full | Small |

SKIN COLORS & LIPSTICK SHADES

Fair Skin   Medium Skin   Tan Skin   Dark Skin

✔ cool skin undertone
/ pinkish beige, light mocha, light mauve

✔ warm skin undertone
/ shell, sand, nude peach

✔ cool skin undertone
/ rosy pink, cranberry, plum, raspberry

✔ warm skin undertone
/ bronze, copper, cinnamon

✔ cool skin undertone
/ light brown, dark berry, brick red

✔ warm skin undertone
/ brick red, brown red, caramel

✔ cool skin undertone
/ dark red, deep plum, ruby red

✔ warm skin undertone
/ honey, ginger, copper bronze

NAILS

NAIL POLISH STEP-BY-STEP

1	2	3	4	5	6	7
Polish along the edge	Apply a dot near the base	Push the dot toward the cuticle	Sweep deliberately ourwards	Continue towards the tip	Repeat on the other side	Sweep straight to the tip

NAIL SHAPES

Oval	Squared Oval	Rounded Rectangle	Square	Round

NAIL ART DESIGNS

Stripes	Polka Dots	Cupcake	French	Modern French

Fade-out Two-toned	Water Marble	Floral	Mosaic	Letter

7.4   # PERFUME

PERFUME CLASSIFICATION

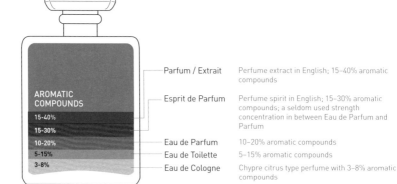

AROMATIC COMPOUNDS

15-40%
15-30%
10-20%
5-15%
3-8%

Parfum / Extrait — Perfume extract in English; 15–40% aromatic compounds

Esprit de Parfum — Perfume spirit in English; 15–30% aromatic compounds; a seldom used strength concentration in between Eau de Parfum and Parfum

Eau de Parfum — 10–20% aromatic compounds

Eau de Toilette — 5–15% aromatic compounds

Eau de Cologne — Chypre citrus type perfume with 3–8% aromatic compounds

PERFUME NOTES

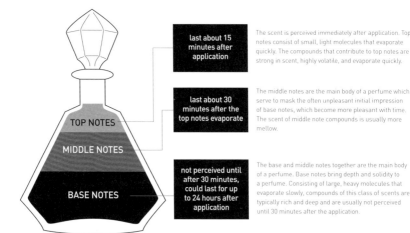

TOP NOTES

MIDDLE NOTES

BASE NOTES

last about 15 minutes after application

The scent is perceived immediately after application. Top notes consist of small, light molecules that evaporate quickly. The compounds that contribute to top notes are strong in scent, highly volatile, and evaporate quickly.

last about 30 minutes after the top notes evaporate

The middle notes are the main body of a perfume which serve to mask the often unpleasant initial impression of base notes, which become more pleasant with time. The scent of middle note compounds is usually more mellow.

not perceived until after 30 minutes, could last for up to 24 hours after application

The base and middle notes together are the main body of a perfume. Base notes bring depth and solidity to a perfume. Consisting of large, heavy molecules that evaporate slowly, compounds of this class of scents are typically rich and deep and are usually not perceived until 30 minutes after the application.

COMMON AROMATIC SOURCES

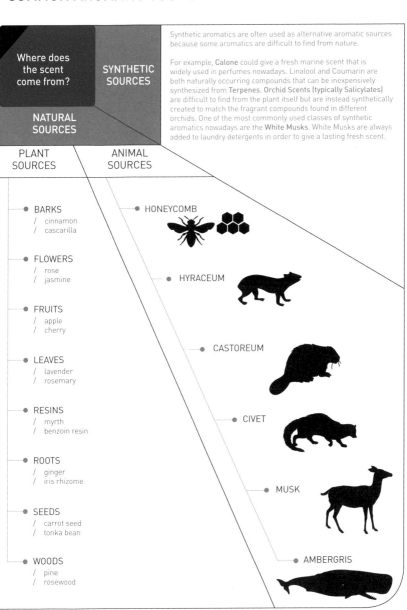

Where does the scent come from?

SYNTHETIC SOURCES

NATURAL SOURCES

Synthetic aromatics are often used as alternative aromatic sources because some aromatics are difficult to find from nature.

For example, **Calone** could give a fresh marine scent that is widely used in perfumes nowadays. Linalool and Coumarin are both naturally occurring compounds that can be inexpensively synthesized from **Terpenes**. **Orchid Scents** (typically Salicylates) are difficult to find from the plant itself but are instead synthetically created to match the fragrant compounds found in different orchids. One of the most commonly used classes of synthetic aromatics nowadays are the **White Musks**. White Musks are always added to laundry detergents in order to give a lasting fresh scent.

PLANT SOURCES

ANIMAL SOURCES

- BARKS
  / cinnamon
  / cascarilla

- FLOWERS
  / rose
  / jasmine

- FRUITS
  / apple
  / cherry

- LEAVES
  / lavender
  / rosemary

- RESINS
  / myrth
  / benzoin resin

- ROOTS
  / ginger
  / iris rhizome

- SEEDS
  / carrot seed
  / tonka bean

- WOODS
  / pine
  / rosewood

- HONEYCOMB

- HYRACEUM

- CASTOREUM

- CIVET

- MUSK

- AMBERGRIS

FASHION IS ARCHITECTURE. IT IS A MATTER OF PROPORTIONS.

/ COCO CHANEL

08 MEASUREMENT AND CARE

8.1 WOMEN'S MEASUREMENT

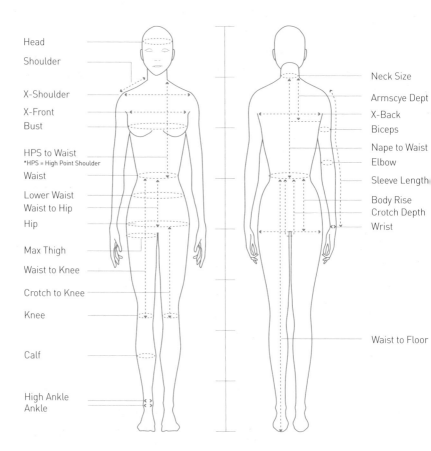

Head
Shoulder
X-Shoulder
X-Front
Bust
HPS to Waist
*HPS = High Point Shoulder
Waist
Lower Waist
Waist to Hip
Hip
Max Thigh
Waist to Knee
Crotch to Knee
Knee
Calf
High Ankle
Ankle

Neck Size
Armscye Dept
X-Back
Biceps
Nape to Waist
Elbow
Sleeve Length
Body Rise
Crotch Depth
Wrist

Waist to Floor

WOMEN'S STANDARD BODY MEASUREMENTS (CM)

										Standard Model
Size (US)	4	6	8	10	12					
Size (UK /Aus)	8	10	12	14	16					
Size (EU / French)	36	38	40	42	44	S	M	L	XL	
Size (Italy)	40	42	44	46	48					
Size (Japan)	7	9	11	13	15					
Bust	82	87	92	97	102	82	84	94	100	84
Waist	64	69	74	79	84	64	70	76	82	66
Lower Waist	82	87	91	96.5	101.5	82	87	91	101.5	84
Hip	88	93	98	103	108	88	94	100	106	91.5
Head	54	56	56	57	58	54	56	57	58	56
Neck Size	35.5	37	38	39.5	40.5	35.5	37	38.5	40	37
Shoulder	12	12.5	12.5	13	13	12	12.5	12.5	13	12.5
X-Shoulder	38	39	40	41	42	38	39	41	42	39
X-Back	33	34.5	35.5	36.5	38	33	34.5	36	37.5	34.5
X-Front	30.5	32	33.5	35	36.5	31	32.5	34	36	32.5
HPS to Waist	42	42.5	43.5	44.5	45	42	42.5	44	46	42.5
Nape to Waist	40.5	41	41.5	42	42.5	39.5	40.5	41.5	42.5	40.5
Armscye Depth	20.4	21	21.5	22	22.5	21.5	22	22.5	23	22
Sleeve Length	57.5	58	58.5	59	59.5	61	63	63.5	64.5	63
Biceps	26.5	27	30	31.5	33	26.5	27	30.5	32.5	27
Elbow	22	22	23	23.5	24	22	22	23	24	22
Wrist	15.5	16	16.5	17	17.5	15.5	16	16.7	17.5	16
Waist to Knee	58	58.5	59	59.5	60	59	59.5	60	61	59.5
Waist to Hip	20	20	21	21.5	21.5	20	20	21	21.5	20
Waist to Floor	103	104	105	106	107	103	104	105.5	107	104
Body Rise	27.5	28	29	29.5	30	27	28	29	30	28
Max Thigh	49.5	52	54.5	57	59.5	49.5	52	56	60	52
Knee	33.5	34.5	36	37	38	33.5	34.5	36.5	38	34.5
Calf	31	32.5	34	35	36	31	32.5	34	36	32.5
High Ankle	20.5	21	21.5	22.5	23	20.5	21	22	23	20.5
Ankle	23.5	24	24.5	25.5	26	23.5	24	25	26	23.5

WOMEN'S NEW EUROPEAN SYSTEM CLOTHING STANDARD SIZES (CM)

Size Code	XS	XS	S	S	M	M	L	L	XL
Bust Girth	76	80	84	88	92	96	100	104	110
Range	74-78	78-82	82-86	86-90	90-94	94-98	98-102	102-107	107-113
Waist Girth	60	64	68	72	76	80	84	88	94
Range	58-62	62-66	66-70	70-74	74-78	78-82	82-86	86-91	91-97
Hip Girth	84	88	92	96	100	104	108	112	117
Range	82-86	86-90	90-94	94-98	98-102	102-106	106-110	110-115	115-120

WOMEN'S STANDARD HAT SIZES (CM)

Size Code	XS	S	S	M	M	L	L	XL	XL
Size (US)	6 5/8	6 3/4	6 7/8	7	7 1/8	7 1/4	7 3/8	7 1/2	7 5/8
Size (UK)	6 1/2	6 5/8	6 3/4	6 7/8	7	7 1/8	7 1/4	7 3/8	7 1/2
Size (EU)	32	34	36	38	40	42	44	46	48
Circumference	52.7	54	55	55.9	56.8	57.8	59	60	60.6

WOMEN'S STANDARD SHOE SIZES (CM)

Size (US)	6	6.5	7	7.5	8	8.5	9	9.5	10
Size (UK)	3	3.5	4	4.5	5	5.5	6	6.5	7
Size (France)	37	37.5	38	38.5	39	39.5	40	40.5	41
Size (Italy)	36	36.5	37	37.5	38	38.5	39	39.5	40
Size (Japan)	23	23.5	24	24	24.5	25	25.5	26	26

8.2 MEN'S MEASUREMENT

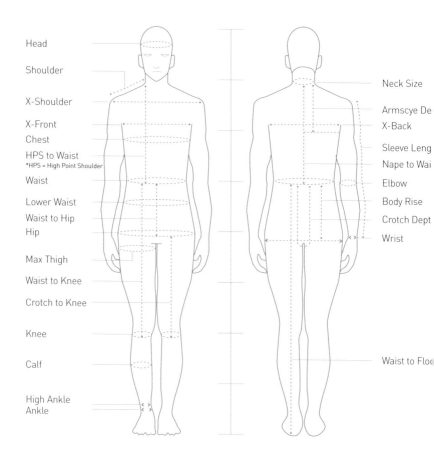

Head
Shoulder
X-Shoulder
X-Front
Chest
HPS to Waist
*HPS = High Point Shoulder
Waist
Lower Waist
Waist to Hip
Hip
Max Thigh
Waist to Knee
Crotch to Knee
Knee
Calf
High Ankle
Ankle

Neck Size
Armscye De
X-Back
Sleeve Leng
Nape to Wai
Elbow
Body Rise
Crotch Dept
Wrist

Waist to Floo

MEN'S STANDARD BODY MEASUREMENTS (CM)

Size (US / UK)	34	36	38	40	40	42	44	46				
Size (EU / France / Italy)	44	46	48	50	50	52	54	56	S	M	L	XL
Size (Japan)	S	S	M	L	L	L	LL	LL				
Head	55	56	57	58	59	60	61	62	55	57	59	61
Neck Size	37	38	40	40	41	42	43	44	38	41	43	45
Chest	88	92	96.5	100	104	108	112	116	92	98	108	116
Waist	74	78	84	86	90	98	102	106	75	83	91	99
Lower Waist	77	81	87.5	89	93	100	104	108	78	86	94	102
Hip / Seat	92	96	99	104	108	114	118	122	94	100	110	118
Shoulder	13	14	15	16	17	18	19	20	14	15	17	20
X-Shoulder	46	47	48	49	50	51	52	53	47	48	50	53
X-Back	41.5	43	44.5	45.5	46.5	47.5	48.5	50.5	42	45	47	50
X-Front	38	40	43	43	44	46	48	50	38	42	45	50
Nape to Waist	42	43	44	45	46	47	48	48	44	44.8	45.6	46.4
Armscye Depth	22	22.8	23.5	24.4	25.2	26	26.4	26.8	23	24.6	26.2	27.8
Sleeve Length	64	66	68	68	69	70	70	70	64	65	66	67
Elbow	24.5	25	25.5	26	26.5	26.5	27	27.5	25	25.5	26	27.5
Wrist	16.4	16.8	17	17.6	18	18.4	18.8	19.2	16.8	17.6	18.4	19.2
Body Rise	26.5	27	27	28	28.4	28.8	29.2	29.6	27	28.5	29.5	30.5
Crotch Length	62	63	65	66.5	68	70	72	73.5	62	66	69	74
Knee	35	36	37	38.5	40	41	42	43	35	38	40	43
Calf	35.5	36.5	37.5	39	40.5	41.5	42.5	43.5	35.5	38	40.5	44
High Ankle	22	22.5	23	23.5	24	24.5	25	25.5	22	23	24	25
Ankle	24.5	25	25.5	26	26.5	27	27.5	28	24.5	25	26	28

MEN'S NEW EUROPEAN SYSTEM CLOTHING STANDARD SIZES (CM)

Size Code	XS	XS	S	S	M	M		L		L
Chest Girth	84	88	92	96	100	104	108	112	116	120
Range	82-86	86-90	90-94	94-98	98-102	102-106	106-110	110-114	114-118	118-123
Waist Girth	72	76	80	84	88	92	96	100	104	108
Range	70-74	74-78	78-82	82-86	86-90	90-94	94-98	98-102	102-106	106-111

MEN'S STANDARD HAT SIZES (CM)

Size Code	XS	S	S	M	M	L	L	XL	XL
Size (US)	6 5/8	6 3/4	6 7/8	7	7 1/8	7 1/4	7 3/8	7 1/2	7 5/8
Size (EU)	32	34	36	38	40	42	44	46	48
Size (UK)	6 1/2	6 5/8	6 3/4	6 7/8	7	7 1/8	7 1/4	7 3/8	7 1/2
Circumference	52.7	54	55	55.9	56.8	57.8	59	60	60.6

MEN'S STANDARD SHOE SIZES (CM)

Size (US)	4	4.5	5	5.5	6	6.5	7	7.5	8	8.5	9	9.5	10	10.5	11
Size (UK / Australia)	3	3.5	4	4.5	5	5.5	6	6.5	7	7.5	8	8.5	9	9.5	10
Size (EU / France/ Italy)	37	37.5	38	38.5	39	39.5	40	40.5	41	41.5	42	42.5	43	43.5	44
Size (Japan)	22	22.5	23	23.5	24	24.5	25	25.5	26	26.5	27	27.5	28	28.5	29

8.3 CARE LABELING

AMERICAN | EUROPEAN

WASH

AMERICAN

Machine wash cycles

Normal | Permanent press | Gentle | Handwash (40°C)

Water temperature

95°C	70°C	60°C	50°C	40°C	30°C
•••	•••	•••	•••	••	•
200°F	160°F	160°F	120°F	100°F	65-85°F

EUROPEAN

Normal | Mild | Very mild | Handwash

Max 95°C	Max 60°C	Max 40°C	Max 30°C
95	60	40	30

BLEACH

AMERICAN

Any bleach | Chlorine bleach | Only non chlorine bleach | Do not bleach

EUROPEAN

Any bleach | Chlorine bleach | Only non chlorine bleach | Do not bleach

IRON

AMERICAN

Any temperature | High | Medium | Low | No steam | Do not iron

EUROPEAN

Max 200°C | Max 150°C | Max 110°C | Do not iron

DRY CLEAN

AMERICAN

(A) | (P) | (F) | ⊗

Any solvent | Any solvent except trichloroethylene | Petroleum solvent only | Do not dry clean

No steam | Low heat | Short cycle | Reduced moisture

EUROPEAN

(W) | (F) | (P)

Wet cleaning | Hydrocarbons process | Tetrachloroethene & solvent listed on symbol F

Mild process | Very mild process | Do not dry clean

DRY

AMERICAN

Tumble dry cycles

Normal | Permanent press | Gentle | Line dry | Do not tumble dry

Tumble dry heat setting

Any heat | No heat | High | Medium | Low | Dry flat | Drip dry

EUROPEAN

Medium Max 80°C | Low Max 60°C | Do not tumble dry

OTHER

AMERICAN

Dry in the shade | Do not dry | Do not wring

JAPANESE

Normal

Gentle

Handwash

95
Max 95°C

60
Max 60°C

40
Max 40°C

30
Max 30°C

Chlorine-based bleaching

Do not bleach

Max 180-210°C

Max 140-160°C

Max 80-120°C

Cover with cloth

Do not iron

Perchloroethylene or petroleum solvent only

Petroleum solvent only

Do not dry clean

Hang & drip dry

Hang & drip dry in the shade

Lay down to dry

Wring gently

Do not wring

CHINESE

Normal

Mild

Very mild

Handwash

Max 95°C

Max 70°C

Max 60°C

Max 50°C

Max 40°C

Max 30°C

Any bleach

Only non chlorine bleach

Do not bleach

Max 200°C

Max 150°C

Do not iron

Wet cleaning

Hydrocarbons process

Tetrachloroethene & solvent listed on symbol F

Mild process

Very mild process

Do not dry clean

Medium Max 80°C

Low Max 60°C

Do not tumble dry

Hang dry

Hang & drip dry

Dry flat

Flat & drip dry

Away from sunlight

8.4 **FABRIC CARE**

WASH

COTTON
Machine wash
at all temperatures

WOOL
Machine wash
at cold temperatures

Handwash

SILK
Machine wash
at cold temperatures

Handwash

LINEN
Machine wash
at all temperatures

POLYESTER/ NYLON
Machine wash
at warm temperatures

VISCOSE/ RAYON
Machine wash
at cold temperatures

LYCRA/ SPANDEX
Machine wash
on normal cycle

ACETATE
Machine wash
at cold temperatures

RAMIE
Machine wash
at cold temperatures

DRY

COTTON
Dry at any
temperature

WOOL

Do not
use dryer

Dry flat

Do not
wring

SILK
Do not
use dryer

Do not
wring

LINEN
Dry at low
temperatures

POLYESTER/ NYLON
Tumble dry
on low

Line dry

VISCOSE/ RAYON
Do not
use dryer

Do not
wring

Line dry

LYCRA/ SPANDEX
Tumble dry
low

ACETATE
Do not
use dryer

Do not
wring

RAMIE
Tumble dry
on low

Do not
wring

Line dry

⊟ IRON

CAUTION

Iron at any temperature
or hang dry

- ! Do not bleach except for
  white garments
- ! Overbleaching can cause
  yellowing and damage

Steam only

- ! Do not bleach
- ! Do not use hot water
- ! Do not use fabric
  conditioner

Steam or iron at low temperatures;
Press inside-out

- ! Do not bleach
- ! Do not use hot water
- ! Do not use dryer

Iron when damp

- ! Do not bleach except for
  white garments
- ! Overbleaching can cause
  yellowing and damage

Steam or press on low to
medium heat

- ! Do not bleach

Steam and turn inside-out

- ! Do not bleach
- ! Do not use hot water
- ! Do not use vinegar

Steam or iron at low temperatures

- ! Do not use dryer sheets

Iron when damp

- ! Do not use starch

Steam or iron at low temperatures

- ! Do not use hot water
- ! Do not use fabric
  conditioner

GLOSSARY

Abrasion Level
/ The degree of desired fraying and wearing on a garment achieved by stone abrasion during wash. Usually the heaviest at the thickest seams, such as the fly, pocket and hem.

Abrasion Resistance
/ The capacity to which a fabric sample can endure different forms of abrasion and friction commonly experienced during regular wear, such as surface rubbing and chafing.

Acceptable Quality Level
/ (AQL) An inspection benchmark for acceptance sampling, which indicates the highest tolerable percentage of defects amongst the lot submitted for sampling. MIL-STD-105E, ISO 2859-1 (1999).

Acceptance Quality Limit
/ (AQL) An inspection benchmark for acceptance sampling, which indicates the maximum tolerable average number of defective items amongst the lot submitted for sampling. ANSI/ASQC Z1.4-2003.

AQL
/ May refer to two different definitions depending on the context. See: **Acceptable Quality Level** and **Acceptance Quality Limit**.

Artwork
/ Designs or illustrations used for textile ornamentation purposes, commonly in the form of printing, weaving or embroidery. These works of art are often purchased from outsourced artists or specialty studios, and are usually unique and exclusive to the purchaser. 'Confined' designs are those picked from a manufacturer's range and made exclusive to a customer.

Bar Tack

/ A series of hand- or machine-made stitches that reinforce specific parts of a garment, such as pocket openings and the bottom of a fly opening, which are commonly subject to stress.

Blind Hem
/ A type of hem finishing where the hem is turned up and secured with stitches that are barely visible from the right side of the garment. Can be done by hand or machine.

Bonding or Laminating
/ A textile treatment that involves fusing or applying a secondary layer of material, often nonwoven, to the primary textile to alter its hand-feel and/or functionality. Examples of common secondary materials: Polyurethane (for water resistance), foam (adds bulk and insulation), etc.

Bow
/ A fabric condition caused by the displacement of knitted courses (or filling yarns) from a line perpendicular to the selvages, resulting in one or more wavy arcs across the width of the textile. Similar conditions may occur in woven fabrics as a result of incorrect finishing.

Breaking Strength
/ The maximum tension that a material specimen can withstand in a tensile testing before it tears.

Burnout / Voided or Devoré
/ Textile techniques used for creating a pattern or design, in which areas of fiber are removed while leaving a fine woven or knitted supporting structure, so that certain elements of the fabric appear translucent and some areas remain solid. This can be done by dissolving specific fibers on the textile using special chemicals to achieve the desired design. Alternatively, it can be done by using a secondary layer of the fabric with the reverse of the design cut away and then applying the chemicals to burn away the pattern.

Burn Test
/ A test conducted to determine the fiber content by burning a swatch, yarn or fibers from a textile sample. Factors including the flammability, smell and quality of the residual ash or melted 'bead' serve as indicators as to the true nature of the fiber or blend.

Bursting Strength
/ The maximum degree of force or pressure that a textile can endure before it bursts when subjected to force applied at right angles to the plane of the textile.

Care Instructions
/ A set of directions which states the appropriate care practices to maintain a product without adverse effect, as well as warning of those practices which are expected to potentially damage the product. The instructions cover washing, drying, dry cleaning and ironing.

Certificate of Origin
/ (CO) An important trade document that attests the country of origin of the goods in question. This certificate is required in the USA and some other countries for tariff purposes.

Circular Knitting
/ A type of machine knitting which produces a knitted 'fabric' in the form of a tube. The fabric, which is knit on a circular knitting bed controlled by separate or sets of needles (called cylinders and dials), can be cut open and finished as a piece of flat fabric or left in its original tubular form, and is usually cut-and-sewn. Nowadays, many circular knitting machines are interfaced with computers and can create elaborate jacquard or fancy stitch patterns, although they are unable to create separate panels to desired sizes and shapes or create 'cable' patterns.

CMT
/ Abbreviation for 'Cut, Make and Trim'. A price jargon used in the apparel industry, referring to the preliminary cost charged by the

contractor for completing the three critical steps of garment production: cutting the fabric, sewing and assembling the components, and finishing the garment, including trimming, embellishing, pressing and labeling.

CO / See: **Cerificate of Origin**

Color Approval / A process in garment production where lab dips or print strike-offs are presented to a customer for approval or rejection, and to gather their comments for further correction. Common errors reflected in these comments include discrepancies in hue, chroma (saturation/intensity) and value (lightness/darkness), etc.

Color Change / Undesirable change in any of the color characteristics, such as the hue, chroma, lightness, or any combination of the above. The color distortion can be detected by comparing the test specimen in question with an untested specimen from a matching fabric or material.

Color Combo, Colorway, Color Pitch / Various ways of describing distinct color combinations used in a textile design or pattern, applicable to all types of patterns including prints, plaids, multi-color jacquards, etc. The related term 'pitch colors' means to conceive new color palettes for a design based on the original one in an artwork or swatch.

Colorfastness / The ability of a material to resist change in any of its color characteristics, transferral of its colorants to other materials (see: **crocking**), or both, due to any environmental factors it may encounter during any stage from manufacturing, testing, storage, to use.

Content / The breakdown of the primary fabric's fiber contents in terms of percentage, e.g. 70% Wool, 30% Silk. The duty rates of imported garments or fabrics will be determined by this content.

Contractor / A company or individual that supplies designated materials, labor or a product package with a contractual agreement of a specified sum and time frame.

Converter / A company or individual that converts greige goods into a finished textile through one or more procedures, such as bleaching, dyeing, printing, brushing, bonding, shrinking, etc.

Counter Sample / A specimen provided by the vendor at the pre-production stage for comments, approval or confirmation on various attributes of the garment, such as the fit and sizing, execution, interpretation of a design or model.

Country of Origin / The country in which garments or other products were manufactured or assembled. This information is required on the garment label.

Cover Stitch

A type of cover stitch : 2-needle lockstitch

/ A type of seam finishing where the raw edges are topstitched on one or both surfaces, so that they are totally bound and enclosed by the threads. The appearance may vary according to the type of stitch and number of threads used.

Crocking / A colorant transferral phenomenon mainly caused by rubbing a colored yarn or fabric onto the surface of another fabric or an adjacent area of the same fabric.

Cross Dye / A dyeing technique that can be used to create speciality effects on a fabric comprising two or more different types of fibers. The special dyestuff used can only be absorbed by one of the fibers within the textile, resulting in heathered, iridescent finishes, or 'yarn dye' effects such as oxford weaves and gingham plaids.

Cubic Feet / The dimensions, namely length x width x height, of the shipment carton. This measurement is required for overshipments.

Customer Owned Goods (COG) / Commodity or material purchased by a customer. This can also be a Repair Claim when the merchandise needs to be sent back to the vendor for repair.

Cuttable Width / The usable width of a piece of fabric - essentially the width of the textile minus the woven edge, selvages or where the finish does not cover the full width of the fabric. An important factor that determines the fabric yield.

Cut-and-Sew / A contractor or factory specializing in cutting and sewing knitted textile and trims, usually in yardages instead of fully-fashioned panels. Due to knitted fabrics' elastic or stretch qualities, special attention to the pattern layout and fabric cutting is required during cut-and-sew procedures, in addition to specialized sewing equipment for construction and finishing.

Cutter's Must / An itemized list of important information required for the production of a garment during the cutting stage, including laying out and cutting the fabric. The information on a Cutter's Must document includes: Directions

Cutter's Must (cont'd) and information for sewing and construction; all the pattern pieces for the body fabric, components and linings; main measurements; and the yields for all textiles and trims.

Cutting Ticket / A working document established by a contractor or manufacturer which lists the production details for a certain order. Much like a Work Order, it covers information such as the customer, style number, quantity, textile and trim details, etc.

Dart

/ A sewn element in garments that can help shape the fit or silhouette, or alternatively used as a decorative feature. It is a wedge or diamond-shaped piece removed from the garment's body, done by solely stitching or by cutting then stitching.

Dimensional Change / The discrepancy in the dimension, including the length and width, of a garment or textile sample when subject to certain conditions. Usually conveyed as a percentage of the sample's initial dimension.

Dog Ear / It is a short diagonal line sewn on the pocket corners. Adding small triangles to the corners will reinforce the pocket and prevent it from separating from the garment.

Double-Bed (Vee) Knitting / A form of machine knitting carried out on two flat beds of knitting needles facing each other, each in control of a stitch during the construction process. Often used for full-fashion knitting and complex stitch combinations, double-bed machines are capable of producing high density knits, such as rib construction, and are the only way of producing true 'cable stitches'.

Drape / The way a piece of fabric hangs or falls, which reflects the visual structure or aesthetic of the textile when made into a garment. Ways of describing the drape: soft, graceful, fluid, crisp, heavy, stiff, bouffant, etc.

Dry Cleaning / A way of cleaning fabrics using organic solvents without any water. Common dry cleaning solvents include fluorocarbons, petroleum solvents, and perchloroethylene. The dry cleaning process requires adding detergent and moisture to the solvent in an environment of up to 75% relative humidity, and hot tumble-drying at 71°C (160°F).

Dyer / Dye House / A converter specializing in dyeing fabrics according to customers' requirements. Offered in a wide spectrum of colors, dyes are chemicals that work by penetrating and bonding with the fibers of a fabric to give it color, the permeance of which depends on various factors, including the fiber, the dyestuff, the 'setting' process and environmental conditions. Dyes usually have no effect on the weight or hand of the textile.

Ease / In fitting and styling, ease refers to a garment's amount of extra 'room' that allows for comfort, movement or enhances appearance.
In sewing, when two pieces of textiles or trims of varying lengths are joined together, with the longer piece 'held in' against the shorter piece with relative smoothness and free from any obvious rushing, pleating or wrinkling along the seam. This type of ease helps shape the garment without the use of extraneous darts or seams as compared to tailoring.

Edge Stitch / A type of edge finishing where a line is stitched parallel just near the folded edge.

Electronic Jacquard / A form of computerized jacquard that uses circular or flat knitting machines to create various fancy patterns and stitches. The computer interface makes it easy for the designer to quickly draft and plan the fashioning or shaping of the garment panels.

Ex-Works (Ex-factory) / A type of shipping arrangement where the seller only bears minimum responsibility, while the buyer takes ownership of the commodity right after it is exported from the seller's facility. In an Ex-works transaction, a seller is only responsible for making the goods available for pick-up at their warehouse or facility and delivering them to the buyer's freight fowarder. Henceforth, the buyer needs to handle all other arrangements, such as insurance, export clearance and other documentation.

Facing / Panels or sections of a piece of extra fabric, always using the outer fabric, that is sewn-in inwards facing the body. Used for creating a clean-finished edge, opening or for concealing the interior construction of a garment.

Fashioning Marks / In knitting, fashioning marks are usually found near the seams in fully-fashioned garments as an indication to where each section was knitted to shape. See: **Fully-fashioned**.

Fiber Content / The percentage breakdown of the fiber contents of a woven or knitted garment's primary, outer or decorative fabric. This information must be included in the garment label together with the care instructions and country of origin, as mandated by the U.S. government.

Filament Yarn / A lengthy and potentially

continuous fiber yarn created through 'extrusion', a process where plastic elements, such as polyester, are pushed through small spinnerets and form filaments as they solidify. While filament yarns are usually man-made, they can also exist in natural forms, such as silk.

Finish (Fabric) / Any special or customer-specified finishing or treatment of a fabric, which may involve improving the color, look or feel of the fabric.

Finisher / A convertor who 'finishes' a textile pre-garment production in one or more of the following ways: Brushing, napping, bleaching, dyeing, printing, glazing, water repellence, etc.

Fit Model / A person whose body measurements represent the standard or sample size or a garment style for development or production purposes. Fashion designers or manufacturers test their garments on a fit model prior to production, to examine the style, fit, drape, movement and comfort of the design on a real person.

Flammability / A material's ease of kindling and ability to support combustion. Fabric flammability is a particularly important issue in the manufacturing of childern's sleepwear and special uniforms.

Flat Knitting / A type of knitting which produces a flat knitted 'fabric' on a single or double-needle bed machine, where a 'carriage' feeds the yarns back and forth across the knitting bed, forming loop-like stitches needle by needle. This technique is considerably slower than circular knitting, but offers more versatility and is often able to fully fashion a garment.

Flats / Design sketches created for use as working diagrams during product development. Technical and free from artistic flourishes, flats include all the detailed information required, including the front and back views of the garment laid flat on a table, special details and treatments, measurements with indication of detail placements, exact proportions, etc.

Fleece / A fabric of natural or man-made fibers, either warp or weft knitted, that is given a plush finish by brushing the loops or floats on one or both surfaces. Its unbrushed form is called French terry.

Structure of French terry

Float Jacquard / A type of fancy knit technique in which yarns are carried on the back of the fabric (floats) and subsequently knitted onto the surface to create a multi-colored pattern or design. It is less firm and bulky as double jacqurd.

Floor Ready / Merchandise that has been received, tagged and is ready to be placed on the selling floor.

Fly closure / One-piece fly: The fly body is extended to form the fly facing, with the extension folded back to create the fly or lapped zipper application. The fly extension is single-ply and usually finished with an over edge seam.
Two-piece fly: The fly or lapped zipper application is formed by a separate piece of fabric. The fly extension is double-ply and folded at the outside edge.

French fly: Also known as 'waist stay', a French fly is an extension applied to the right side of the fly stand, allowing for a concealed extra button closure.

Folder (Operation) / A sewing machine attachment that folds multiple layers of fabric and garment parts together, saving the need for the machine operator to manually do so during the assembly stage. Its functions include: binding, hemming, flat-felling seams, and attaching plackets, etc.

Freight Chargeback / A freight deduction, fine or penalty levied by the customer against the supplier. There are two types of freight chargebacks:
Agreement: The supplier or vendor consents to sharing the freight charge.
Violation: The supplier or vendor bears the full freight charges as well as an extra handling fee. This usually occurs due to violation of the Purchase Order Contract, or the agreed-upon carrier or routing selection.

Fully Fashioned / A technical term in knitting which indicates that each individual section of the garment is 'fashioned' or shaped to its finished dimensions for every size within the range of the design. These sections are then usually looped or linked together to create the finished product. Fully-fashioned garments are more cost-efficient because it wastes less yarn.

Garment Twist / Also known as torquing or spiralling, a garment twist is when the woven or knitted fabric panels

Garment Twist (cont'd) of a garment are rotated or twisted, usually laterally, due to latent stress released during laundering.

Garment Wash / The washing of dyed garments to tone down the color, create a worn, weathered, distressed look or seam abrasion, or to soften the fabric.

Gauge / A technical term in knitting which indicates the number of needles (wales) per inch on the knitting machine bed (or needles per 1-1/2" for some full fashioned knitting equipment), hence the fineness of the resulting fabric. The higher the gauge number, i.e. the more needles per inch, the finer the knitted fabric.

Grade Rule / A standardized amount of increases or decreases to the measurements of the garment patterns within the designated size range. This usually reflects the standard 'fit' of their customers, and can be set up or revised by the designer, contractor or the retailer.

Grading / A crucial step in garment production, grading refers to the proportional increase or decrease of the dimensions of all the sections of a model garment, sample or proto, based on the full intended production size range for a certain style. This step ensures proper fit across all sizes in the range, and helps determine the cutting layout (marker) for the textile, trims and other components.

Grain / A textile term used in woven textiles to describe the direction in which woven threads run.
Straight grain: Threads running along the length of the textile, parallel to the selvage.
Cross grain: Threads running across the width of the textile.
Bias grain: The 45 degree angle diagonal thread line across the textile.
Off grain: When the straight grain and cross grain are not at straight angles with each other or as indicated for the pattern piece.

Greige (Grey) Goods / Fabrics from a mill or knitter that are fresh off the loom, raw and unfinished. Greige goods must be followed up with a series of finishing procedures, such as bleaching, dyeing, printing, brushing, etc.

Hand (Handfeel) / The characteristics of the textile perceived by touch, such as soft, stiff, harsh and bouncy. It plays an important part when deciding the choice of fabric for creative design or production based on the specified quality.

Inspection Certificate / A document issued by independent testing organizations as an authoritative quality guarantee, verifying that the merchandise is in good condition and meets relevant standards before it is shipped.

Interfacing / Commonly used on collars, cuffs, front plackets, hems and lapels, it is a woven or nonwoven layer placed between the upper and lower fabrics to maintain the shape, durability and wrinkle-resistance for the garment. Fusible interfacings are attached to a garment piece by ironing at a high temperature in order to temporarily melt the heat-sensitive adhesive for an affixable property. It is relatively more long-lasting unless the clothing is subjected to the same level of heat.
Sew-in Interfacings are attached to a garment piece by stitching so that it 'floats' between the upper and lower fabrics for enhanced maneuverability. It does not change the appearance of fabrics, yet it adds support to the clothing.

Interlining / A material applied between the upper and lower fabrics in designated areas of a garment to provide additional weight and warmth for enhanced functionality.

Jobber / A textile supplier that sells within the fashion industry rather than to the public, who buys overruns, mill ends and unused sample yardage from manufacturers, mills and importers, then resells them to wholesalers, small-scale garment manufacturers and retailers.

Knit-down / A sample piece of knitted fabric often used for approval purposes before the production of a garment. It is used as a demonstration of certain color, yarn, stitch or pattern combinations.

Lab Dips / Pieces of sample fabrics colored by dyers, spinners or printers to present to a customer for approval of the coloration. Accepted ones will serve as the standard of production, whereas rejected ones will require comments for correction.

Lead Time / The amount of time required for the completion of a product development, including design, prototype, approval, counter sample and production.

Ligne (Buttons) / A measurement unit of length used by watch- and button-makers before the metric system was adopted. 20 lignes is equal to 0.5 inches and 40 lignes is equal to 1 inch.

Line Plan / Set by and for the design team, it is a schedule that provides a framework of product development for the coming seasonal collection. Merchandizing teams will outline styles and SKU count of the collection based on categories, which is usually based on the sales analysis from previous seasons.

Lining / A layer of fabric attached to the skin-facing side of a garment in order to conceal the interior construction such as seams and stitches. Types of lining include full, half, quarter and no lining.

Linking or Looping / Performed by skilled machine operators, it is a labor-intensive assembly technique mostly used in high-end knit apparel. The process joins pieces of flat knits together by applying a flexible, elastic chain-stitch seam to which the two fabrics meet.

Links-Links / A knitting technique in which purl stitches and regular stitches are applied on the same wale to create a thick rib effect for ample stretch quality.

Manufacturer ID / A multi-digit code that represents a vendor that is used in the Universal Product Code (UPC) system.

Marker / A comprehensive diagram indicating the placement of all graded paper patterns whose shapes will be cut out in a piece of fabric for the most economical use of textiles. Sketched manually or with the aid of a computer, it must take all variables into consideration including matching prints, patterns and grain lines.

Matching (Match Points) / Commonly used at the front of armscye, across the placket and along the seam, it is a technique of making various repetitive elements such as prints, stripes, plaids or embellishments transition seamlessly across two pieces of fabrics for a balanced visual of the pattern. It requires additional cost and time, and hence is considered a sign of high quality.

Migration / An irregular transfer or distribution of dyes, pigments or any other materials from one part of the fabric to another in the form of bleeding, crocking, etc.

Mill / A supplier specializing in spinning yarn or weaving textiles. A vertical mill streamlines its services from spinning to finishing of the fabric and subsequently selling it to the market.

Minimums / The lowest limit of order set by a vendor or mill when selling products. It is usually measured in fabric yardage, poundage or by pieces.

Muslin (Toile) / An inexpensive unbleached cotton fabric that is used to create the prototype of a design in order to test the fit and proportion. It can be written with construction remarks. After the initial prototype is formed, it is often taken apart for sampling, patternmaking, and approximating the fabric choice.

Notch

Notches on sleeve cap
/ The cut-in markings on paper patterns or slopers that locate the positions of various sewing constructions such as seam allowances, gathering, cutting, etc.

Package (Production) / A tying purchase agreed by a contractor on behalf of the customer, where it buys all piece goods and trims in addition to CMT (Cut, Make and Trim) services.

Packing List / A list of products and their quantities that will be packed for shipping.

Piece (of Fabric) / A bolt or roll of cloth whose length is determined by actual manufacturing or production processes.

Plating / A knitting process where two different types of yarns are simultaneously used - one on the upper side and one on the lower side. Aesthetically it gives a heathered effect. It also adds practicality to the fabric if a stretch or high-performance yarn is knitted on the back of a fabric for enhanced elastic, absorbent, moisture-wicking or anti-rash qualities.

Pleat

Box pleat
/ A fold of fabrics performed on garments for expending or styling purposes. Types of pleats include forward, reverse, knife, box, inverted, accordion, etc.

Pocketing / A fabric used in the making of pouches of a garment. It is usually different from the shell fabric, and is in general sturdier and more lightweight.

Pre-Production / Pre-production processes held before bulk production. It constructs garments using the actual production patterns, sewing line and machinery. After that, it will immediately be followed by bulk production.

Pre-Production (P/P) Sample / After the approval of the sales sample, another batch of samples will be produced. They must be made of ctual fabrics and produced by the factory who will be in charge of bulk production. When they are approved, bulk production will commence.

Pressing / One of the manufacturing processes, it is performed by ways of heating or steaming the fabric with

Pressing (cont'd) irons or machines, so as to enhance the smoothness, structure or create permanent creases on a garment. Hard press: Creates permanent creases and long-lasting shapes. Soft press: Removes wrinkles of the fabric for a smooth appearance but it does not create permanent creases.

Prototype (Proto) / An initial sample of a given design. It can be made of muslin or any available fabric as it is solely for assessment.

Punch (Mark) / A small hole on a paper pattern that will transfer various sewing constructions marked on the paper pattern to the fabric.

Racking / A basic function of a knitting machine where stitches are transferred from one needle to another to form a zigzag pattern. It is also one of the steps of making cable stitches on a double bed machine.

Rib Knit (Ribbing) / Usually seen on the placket or hem of a garment, it is an elastic textile achieved by alternating jersey and purl stitches that create a vertical ribbed effect.

Sales Sample / The exact replica of a retail product used by the salesperson for wholesaling purpose.

Sample Cut (Yardage) / Yardage of fabric purchased from a mill for sales and product development. Mills will only manufacture fabrics in limited colors. If a customized colorway is requested, a surcharge is required for producing sample fabrics. Alternatively, a customer can take a portion of fabrics from bulk production and use it as sample cuts.

Sample Loom / A sample yardage given by the mill for customer's approval or comments. A surcharge is usually required.

Sample Room / Set alongside with a design studio or in a contractor's property, it is a place where protos, counter and sales samples are made.

Sample / A product that is not for resale. Rather it serves as a selling tool (called sales sample), a guide for development (called counter samples) or a standard for production (called top-of-production).

Sanding / Sand Wash / An intentional abrasion performed on a garment for aesthetic purpose. Initially it was achieved with a high-pressure sand blaster, now it is done by washing in chemicals, or gritting with a dry brush.

Seam Allowance / It sets the distance between the stitching and the edge of a fabric. It prevents the seam from slipping, bursting or fraying.

Seam Slippage / Caused by stress or straining, it is

found when the yarn shifts or slips out of stitching, causing an open seam or fabric distortion.

Seconds / Fabrics that contain excessive defects, damage or irregularities and thus are not of the highest quality. Considered as flawed, they cannot be marketed at full prices.

Selvage / A self-finished edge that runs along the warp threads. It keeps the woven fabric from ravelling and thus making it more durable. Since the fabric is stabilized by the process, it then can undergo further finishing processes.

Shading / A gradual change in hue, chroma or lightness in vertical or horizontal direction. It is considered a defect if unintended, but it adds aesthetic values to a design if it is done on purpose and is called ombré or dégradé.

Shrinkage / A decrease in length or width of a fabric or a garment achieved by contacting with water, heat, steam or wet-cleaning.

Single Needle (Construction) / A superior stitching technique that is normally used in high-end menswear garments. It sews a row of stitches along both the upper and bottom side of a seam, with only the upper one being visible. On the contrary, Double Needle Construction sews two parallel rows of stitches and is considered less durable.

Size Run / Samples of garments in all sizes made prior to mass production in order to ensure that all sizes are accurate.

Skew / Considered an improper finishing, it refers to the displacement of knitted or woven courses that forms a line perpendicular to the edge of a fabric.

Sloper / Also known as a block pattern, it is a thick piece of paper or cardboard used to sculpt the basic design of a garment whose fit and appearance have already been approved. It is used for further development of more complex styles or paper patterns.

Spec. Sheet (Specs) / A document that lists the complete specifications of a garment of an accessory made before production. It includes a brief illustration, measurement chart or any relevant information for the manufacturer or Quality Control.

Special Finish / Additional treatments performed on a textile for certain functional or aesthetic purposes, such as water-, stain- and wrinkle-resistance, odor-blocking, UV protection etc.

Stain / A spot of dirt or discoloration on a fabric or any base material that is difficult to remove by laundering or

Standard (Color)
dry cleaning.
/ They are submitted to a mill as the standard for production. The mill will then provide lab dips or strike-offs for approval or comments before mass production or further adjustments.

Stay
/ A strip of material applied on the interior of a garment in order to prevent stretching or distortion. It is a stabilization treatment to maintain the shape or detail of the construction.

Stitches per Inch
/ The optimal density of stitches in garment construction. It varies depending on the component, fabric, design or durability of a garment.

Stock/Bulk
/ Fabrics that are manufactured strictly for mass production as opposed to sample production.

Store Pack
/ A package that will be shipped to the retailer. It is packed by style, color or size.

Tearing Strength
/ The force required to continue ripping a previously torn fabric.

Tech Package
/ Also known as Spec Package, it is a compilation of technical specifications sent to a factory for every new product. It includes Sketch Sheet, Specification Measurement Sheet, Fabric and Trim Sheet, etc.

Time and Action Calendar
/ A seasonal calendar set to keep design, merchandizing, production and sales divisions at their highest efficiency so that they will be in sync with one another throughout production and retail processes.

Top of Production (Top of Line)
/ The first batch of products completed by production line for quality check purpose. After approval, it will be immediately followed by bulk production.

Topstitch Gauge
/ It measures the distance between two parallel rows of topstitching, which is called double-needle topstitch.

Topstitching
/ Usually seen on the outer edge of a garment, it is a row of stitching shown on the shell fabric for functional, structural or aesthetic purposes. It can attach a garment section to another, and keep garment pieces in place.

Transfer
/ A basic function of a double bed knitting machine where stitches are transferred from the front to the back bed of needles or vice versa during the knitting process.

Trim (Trimming)
/ Ornamental details that are applied to a garment for aesthetic purpose. Usually made by a manufacturer or supplier, they can be a wide range of materials including ribbons, patches, lace, braids or piping.

Tuck
/ A knitting technique that a needle holds more than one loop at a time. It causes the stitch to pull up the surrounding stitches in order to

elongate the wale. It is used to achieve certain visual effects or lengthwise elasticity.

Underlining
/ A complete layer or individual panels attached to the back of a shell fabric to lend a garment certain hand or visual effects such as structure, weight or opaqueness.

Under-stitching
/ It effectively prevents the lining or facing from peeking out from the inside of a garment. It is a row of stitching along the inside edge of the facing that allows the shell fabric to roll over and conceal the seam edge.

Union Dye
/ Union dye is a technique in which all the different fibers in a textile are dyed the same color by using appropriate dye chemicals.

Waistband

/ A straight waistband is a flat trim at the waist whose pattern edges are cut on and parallel on the straight grain of fabrics.
A contour waistband was cut differently at the top edge and side seam to ensure that the waistband sits close to the body's curve.
A curtain waistband is supported by a bias strip on the interior of the shell fabric that hangs below the waistline seam. It is commonly used for tailored trousers and skirts.

Washdown
/ A washing, chemical, sourcing or mechanical treatment performed on a fabric or a garment to obtain a worn-in or laundered look.

Wicking
/ A fiber's or a fabric's ability to transport moisture away from the skin in order to enhance evaporation and thus comfort.

Yarn Count
/ A numerical value (usually fraction) which shows the fineness of a yarn and is determined by the relationship between weight and length. New Metric (NM) is a popular count system amongst all, which indicates the diameter of a yarn based on a fixed length.

Yield
/ A means of textile measurement, it represents the length of a fabric or weight of a knitted fabric. It counts as a cost factor in the manufacturing process.

ACKNOWLEDGEMENTS

FASHIONARY

EDITOR-IN-CHIEF & CHAIRMAN
PENTER YIP

EDITOR
MINI MISS MIA

FASHIONARY FASHIONPEDIA SERIES

LAYOUT DESIGNER
STUDIOWMW
MINI MISS MIA

COPY EDITOR
GINNY CHAN

PROOFREADER
GINNY CHAN
GRACE HUNG
VERA CHAN

ILLUSTRATORS BY CHAPTER
CH.1
MINI MISS MIA
VIKKI YAU

CH. 2-3, 5-8
MINI MISS MIA

CH. 4
MINI MISS MIA
SARA CHOW
LILY LAM

CONSULTANTS

CHARLENE WONG
KARMUEL YOUNG
POLLY WU
CAROL TAO
TRAVIS LI
THOMAS KUNG
EILEEN CHAN
ZOE KWOK

HO HO TAK
EUNICE LEE
JOVIA LAI
RONNIE TUNG
ANNIE CHEUNG
MIKE MAK
MIKE CHAN
JESSICA YEUNG